The Aussie dumb a*se

'A Hunter and Gatherer

by Lisa Fitzgerald

Bring out your inner primal!

A have a crack guide to preparing Nature's finest!

Dedication
To all of you who began your cooking journey with The Aussie Dumb A*se Cookbook and are continuing in your quest to broaden your culinary knowledge – two, four, six, eight – keep going, don't wait.

Acknowledgements
Once again to my husband, children, family and friends who encouraged me to tackle book two – I thank you all for your belief and support. I can't believe I am actually doing this again.

To all of you who fronted up again for photos, knowing full well what to expect, and to all the new faces; thank you for allowing me to take advantage of your great sense of Aussie humour. Feel free to spend a lifetime paying me back.

Further thanks must go to my good friend Kerri from Fresh Eyre Photography for helping out with photographs, editing and general support and to my new friend and fellow author Bruce Lindsay. Bruce I thank you sincerely for holding my hand and walking me through the self-publishing minefield that was book one, and for all your continuing encouragement and support. Everyone needs a mentor and I truly could not have done it without you.

Rommie from Hardshell Publishing; your professionalism and work ethic are second to none and a big part of the book's success. Thank you for your many hours of hard work.

And lastly I would like to acknowledge the family members and friends who shared their knowledge and contributed in many aspects of this book.

Copyright © Lisa Fitzgerald 2020
This book is copyright. No part can be used or reproduced in any form without written permission from the author.

For further information and enquiries, please contact:

Farmyard Antics
1304 Butler Centre Road
Tumby Bay SA 5605
Email: farmyardantics@gmail.com
Find us on Facebook: The Aussie Dumb A*se Cookbook

Photography
Bri Hammond – Cover, title and Techniques and Recipes page photography – www.brihammond.com
Kerri Cliff of Fresh Eyre Photography – Herbing it Up, How to Masta Pasta and The Meaty Bits title pages and Kitchen Tool Kit #2 – www.fresheyrephoto.com and Lisa Fitzgerald

Editing
Bruce Lindsay – author of Chamberlain Australian Innovator, Lancia – 70 Years of Trailblazing, Armstrong Siddeley – The Sphinx with the Heart of a Lion, Kerri Cliff of Fresh Eyre Photography and Gladys Lehmann

Illustrations
Lisa and Jae Fitzgerald

Publication design
Hardshell Publishing – www.hardshellpublishing.com

The Aussie Dumb A*se Cookbook 2 'A Hunter and Gatherer's Guide'
First published in 2012
Second edition published in 2020

ISBN: 978-0-9806841-4-8 (Paperback)
ISBN: 978-0-9806841-5-5 (Kindle eBook)

Other Farmyard Antics Publications: The Aussie Dumb A*se Cookbook

Disclaimer: Pregnant women or people with specific dietary considerations should consult their health professionals if in doubt about using any of the recipes in this book. Photographs do not to reflect the personalities or tendencies of the people pictured in this book. Whilst every effort has been made to make sure that the information contained in this book is correct at the time of printing, the author accepts no responsibility for any inaccuracies which may have occurred.

Introduction

Welcome back everyone (and hello to all of you joining me for the first time), and might I say thank you all for taking me on the ride of my life with book one. My humble little home grown creation seemingly found its way to all corners of the globe, including into the hands of the odd musician and celebrity; but most importantly to you.

Since The Aussie Dumb A*se Cookbook was released in 2009 there have been many great success stories to report. It has given me no end of satisfaction to hear of electricians whipping up apple pies after work (and no, it was not my son); Uni students discovering that there is more to food than the drive-through; those horrified that they have so far managed to survive cooking frozen chicken without poisoning themselves (though that could explain their husband's irritable bowel syndrome); and then there were those that have just plain had a go.

Introducing The Aussie Dumb A*se Cookbook 2 'A Hunter and Gatherer's Guide'. For as long as humans have roamed the earth we have had to make the most of what nature has provided in order to survive, and thankfully (at last) society is realising the importance of the return to simple, wholesome food.

This Hunter and Gatherer's Guide Cookbook aims to introduce you to some timeless knowledge and techniques that you may not have previously attempted, or been too embarrassed to ask about. It's all the sort of stuff that Grandma used to do. Each new technique is then backed up with some great recipes to help you on your way to preparing some great meals. Again, I do not profess to be any expert, but merely wish to encourage you to 'have a crack' yourself. My motto continues to be – if it's edible, you've succeeded.

This book dabbles not only into cooking, but other aspects that support it. Many of these I have only learnt myself in recent times through my Kitchen Specialist role at our local school. They are just too good not to share and include how to start your own simple garden. Trust me – it's not too hard and it will encourage and inspire you to use more fresh ingredients. You'll also find lots of extra kitchen tips and advice worth taking on board.

I have heard many inspiring stories from book one, of people who took the plunge and launched themselves into the kitchen, so all I can say is 'while you're on a good thing, stick to it.'

So two four six eight, keep going, don't wait!

Contents

Introduction iii

Kitchen Tool Kit #2 vi

Recipes for Success - The Prenuptials to Cooking 1

Nice Rice 1

Rookie Tips for the Gluten Free Guest 2

Scary Times - Cleaning out the Fridge 4

Taking Stock of Stock Cubes 4

Setting the Table (and the Scene) 5

How to Excel at Garage Sales 7

A Guide to Box Gardening 8

Indoor Seed Propagation 12

Techniques and Recipes .... 13 - 112

Glossary of Aussie Slang #2 114

About the Author 116

Techniques and Recipes

- **Herbing it Up!** 13
  Including a Glossary of Common Herbs

- **How to Masta Pasta** 23
  Learn How to Make Your Own

- **Bread Making for Beginners** 31
  Bread, Pizzas, Hot Cross Buns and More

- **Seafood Made Simple** 37
  Preparing and Cooking the Best we Have to Offer

- **Camping Capers** 59
  Tips, Tricks and Recipes

- **The Meaty Bits** 75
  A Guide to Basic Cuts, Marinades and Recipes

- **The Art of Preserving** 87
  How to Make Nature's Finest Last all Year Round

- **Festive Fare** 101
  A Dumb A*se Guide to Christmas Catering

Kitchen Tool Kit #2

- SLOW COOKER
- PASTA MACHINE 
- DEEP-FRYER 
- SLOTTED METAL SPOON 
- MOULI SIEVE 
- FOOD PROCESSOR 
- OYSTER SHUCKER 
- FISH SCALER 
- FILLETING KNIFE 
- JAFFLE IRON 
- MUM'S OLD FLAT BLADED KNIFE 
- CHRISTMAS PUDDING TIN 
- SMOKE BOX 
- BREAD TIN 
- FRENCH STICK TIN 
- RAVIOLI CUTTER 
- CAKE ICING GUN 
- METAL SIEVE 
- CAMP OVEN 
- TRIVET

Recipes for Success – The Prenuptials to Cooking

I've put together some information on a few things that might benefit your experiences in the kitchen in the longer term. They delve more deeply into produce (like growing your own), equipment and ingredients, as well as offering practical advice. Call them 'Recipes for Success' if you like.

But remember, by no stretch of the imagination do I consider myself to be anything other than a home cook who muddles her way through baking. Every now and then though, you discover some things that are worth sharing, both in and out of the kitchen. So here is my two cents worth.

Nice Rice

Many types of rice are produced around the world, each slightly different. Varieties are largely determined by their length, thickness and levels of starch, flavour and stickiness.

Note: Eating rice off the sand is not recommended – this photo was simply some crazy artistic licence.

As a rule, rice should always be rinsed before cooking to remove any unwanted stuff left over from the fields.

Rice falls into two main categories – white and whole grain. As whole grain rice is less processed, it holds greater flavour and aroma (smell), but needs to be stored in the fridge so it doesn't go off.

BROWN RICE is a form of whole grain rice, where much of the husk of the grain is still intact, therefore it requires a longer cooking time.

WHITE RICE goes through a polishing process and cooks faster. It usually has less flavour and nutritional content, but can be stored normally in the pantry cupboard.

- **Risottos** are usually made with medium-grained rice such as Arborio because it holds its shape well and absorbs flavours.
- **Chinese and Indian** dishes often use long-grained rice such as Basmati.
- **Japanese** cooking often uses Sushi rice which is a short-grained variety that has an increased stickiness to it.
- **Thai** dishes often use Jasmine rice because of its lovely smell.

Fail-Safe Rice (GF)

When it comes to cooking rice, it's all about timing. No matter what technique you use, rice is designed to be served straight after cooking. Therefore it is important to get your time management skills working, as if rice is left to sit for too long, it can become sticky and unpalatable.

My Aunty D shared her fail-safe rice technique with me and it is spot on. Adjust the quantities to suit your own needs but keep the ratios the same.

INGREDIENTS:

- 1 cup of rice of your choice
- Just under 2 cups of hot water
- ½ teaspoon of salt

METHOD:

1. Place rice in a colander and wash under cold running water for a few seconds to remove any yucky stuff. Allow a moment or two to drain.
2. Place rice in a saucepan at least 3 times its size. Add the hot water and salt and turn the element on to high. Have the lid partially on.
3. Bring the rice to the boil and then reduce the heat to a simmer for 5 minutes. Set your timer as this part is important.
4. After rice has boiled for 5 minutes, remove from the heat and place the saucepan lid firmly on. Let sit for another 5 minutes.
5. Fluff rice up gently with a fork and serve immediately. Trust me – it will be perfect every time if served straight away.

Rookie Tips for the Gluten Free Guest

Their Guts Will Thank You! Gluten intolerance is something about which we are hearing more and more these days and fortunately many more products are being labelled 'gluten free' for the consumer.

My brother wanted me to write a gluten free recipe book but I am not sufficiently knowledgeable to do so. I was so naïve that I thought it was only items that listed wheat as an ingredient. However there are several gluten free members in my own family who have forced me out of my cooking comfort zone. Instead I am going to offer some basic rookie tips and a guide to some recipes which I know to be gluten free if someone with an allergy rocks up unexpectedly for dinner.

Of course if you are living with a gluten intolerance then you will have all the books and information you need – this is only a snapshot for the surprise guest.

Look for the adjacent symbol (GF) next to many recipes in this book that are deemed safe for the gluten free guest. Lots of the other recipes can be adapted by purchasing gluten free alternatives such as flours, bread crumbs etc - it's just a matter of trial and error.

VERY GENERAL TIPS

- Always cook the gluten free variety first on the BBQ, frypan etc as the remaining residue from previous food can be a problem.

- If you don't understand or have never heard of the ingredient, be cautious! When shopping you can always use your phone to Google™ whether an ingredient is gluten free or not.

- A real trap I found can be in various commercially bought sauces and condiments so pick one that is labelled gluten free – wine can be tricky and coeliacs should be very careful.

- Be cautious when sugar appears in the ingredients list as it may be sourced from wheat. Sugar cane is OK.

- If a product says wheat free – it may still contain gluten as gluten does not just come from wheat but from many other sources like barley, rye and oats.

- Most deli meats such as ham, beef or turkey will contain gluten, so make sure you buy a brand that clearly states that it is gluten free - it is easiest to find them in the pre-packaged section.

- You can buy gluten free flours (and many other items) which can be substituted in many recipes – it's just a matter of trial and error. Many brands of stock cubes are also labelled gluten free.

- Finally, if having a gluten free guest over for dinner and you are in doubt about any ingredient containing gluten, sometimes it's easiest to just shoot them a text to find out whether they can eat it or not – they'll love your efforts and their guts will thank you for it!

If you need further information, talk to your guest or consult a health professional as some people only have a mild intolerance whilst for others it's a more serious issue.

Scary Times – Cleaning out the Fridge

Now suffice to say, the best practice is to clean out your fridge on a regular basis. A good habit to get into is to remove the dead stuff each time you bring your shopping home.

This is great in theory, though I am a repeat offender when it comes to mouldy stuff in the fridge. Oh sure, I had great intentions for all the magnificent dishes I was going to create with that delicious pumpkin or leek; but at the end of the day, when I open the door my fridge often greets me with an offensive reminder that I have been remiss in my duty as the head cook. It is of some consolation that the chooks reap the benefits of my misdemeanours.

DEALING WITH A SMELLY FRIDGE

- Obviously the first step is to find the offending items in your fridge and remove them. I am assuming there will be more than one.
- Remove the entire contents of your fridge and wipe up any spills and slime with hot water and detergent. This is the perfect time to have a cull.
- Place a squirt of vanilla essence in a bowl of clean water and use a cloth to wipe over all of the shelves. This will add a pleasant smell to your fridge.
- As extra insurance you can place a small, open dish of bicarb soda somewhere inside as this tends to absorb bad odours. (Good trick for the bedroom maybe?)

GENERAL FRIDGE TIPS

- Avoid potential food poisoning by making sure your raw meats are either well wrapped or in plastic containers. These should be stored on the lowest shelf in case of any drips, as these can easily contaminate other foods.
- Buy a cheap but solid tray or basket in which to store some of your condiments. You can then lift the tray out easily to get what you want and avoid having to pull out fifteen different jars to get to the one at the back.

Taking Stock of Stock Cubes

When buying stock cubes, check on the packet how much liquid you need per cube as brands differ.

For example, some brands suggest you use 1 cube to 1 cup of water or liquid while others specify 1 cube to 2 cups. This has a huge bearing on how many you use. My advice is to start with less than you think as you can always add more. If you have used too many, you will have to increase your liquid level which can sometimes compromise the flavour. This is a valuable point which may have led to some confusion in book one, as the amount needed depends on the brand of stock cubes you buy. When in doubt, determining how much liquid content you have in your recipe and checking the instructions for your brand of stock cubes, can help you to work out how many your recipe will require.

Setting the Table (and the Scene)

It never ceases to amaze me how many people do not know how to do this properly, so here it is in both written and pictorial forms.

The table sets the scene when people arrive so it's well worth investing some time and effort. Don't underestimate the 'wow' factor of having a nicely written Menu on the table for your guests, just to get them salivating. With computers these days there is no excuse to not be creative.

Standard table setting is pictured here for you as well as a setting which includes entrée cutlery (see overleaf), but the basic principle for the procedure is that you work from the outside in as the courses progress.

This means that if you start with either soup or entrée, this cutlery will be on the outside, farthest from the plate. A point to note is that regardless of whether someone is left or right-handed, the table is usually set for a right hander.

These table settings offer suggestions for a meal of 2 or 3 courses, but if you really want to impress, and you have the food and the recipes, you can offer a meal of many courses or a 'degustation' menu.

FORK — DESSERT SPOON — KNIFE — SOUP SPOON

The fork (which has *four* letters), sits on the *left* hand side of the plate (which also has *four* letters). If serving an entrée, the smaller fork sits to the left of the larger main course fork.

The knife (which has *five* letters), sits on the *right* hand side of the plate (which has *five* letters also). If serving an entrée the smaller knife sits to the right of the larger main course knife. The blade of the knife should always face the plate.

Soup spoons are placed on the outside of the right hand side cutlery (to the right of the knife/knives). They are on the outside because soup is the first course you would eat.

Dessert spoons are placed on the inside of the knife/knives (closest to the plate on the right hand side), as this is the last piece of cutlery you use on that side. Sometimes a small sweet fork and spoon can be used instead of a large dessert spoon, especially if you are serving something such as a cheesecake or food which may need two utensils to pick it up. I doubt very much you will have a set of these in your possession, but if you do, these are normally positioned at right angles to the other cutlery and above the main plate.

The glass/es are always situated above the knife/knives. The types of glasses you provide will be determined by what you are drinking. For example Champagne glasses are tall and thin, whilst wine glasses are usually shorter and wider. If you don't have any flash glasses, try checking out your local charity shop or garage sale. Here you can grab great gear for next to nothing (see section on Garage Sales).

Side plates sit to the left of the main plate. The main plate may or may not be on the table initially. They look like a miniature main course plate and are usually used for bread or sometimes side salads. These smaller plates are often used for serving entrée as well.

[Image: A place setting labelled with SIDE PLATE, ENTRÉE FORK, MAIN FORK, MAIN PLATE, THE GLASSES, DESSERT SPOON, MAIN KNIFE, ENTRÉE KNIFE, SOUP SPOON]

SERVIETTE FOLDING

I am not going to go into this here, as it can be quite a work of art, but if you want to know more, Google™ it!

COURSE NAMES AND EXPLANATIONS

Any Dumb A*se knows that there is an order in which you serve at a dinner party and this is determined by what you have chosen for your menu. For example in Winter you may choose to serve a soup instead of an entrée; it's usually one or the other, not both. As for the set procedure, one needs to get it right.

- **Pre-dinner nibbles** (optional and obviously come before the start of the dinner). Though not necessary (and somewhat more expensive) many people like to serve a selection of cheeses, dips etc when people are arriving. These are usually served away from the dinner table.

- **Soup** (is generally a Winter option and usually served instead of an entrée). Soup is an easy menu idea that can be pre-prepared and just heated on the night. If you are serving a bread roll with your soup you could place the smaller knife on the side plate instead of to the right of the main knife. If you don't have an entrée you would also then omit the entrée fork.

- **Entrée** (a French word pronounced 'ontray'). An entrée is a petite-sized tasting, usually served on a smaller plate such as a side plate, depending on what it is. You would generally serve either a soup or an entrée, rarely both.

- **Main** (the main meal of the evening).

- **Dessert** Ooh yes please, and don't misspell it or you will end up with desert.

- **Either Coffee and Chocolates or a Small Cheese Plate** to nibble away for the rest of the night.

TABLE SERVICE

The rule for table service is that you deliver meals to your guests' right hand side and retrieve dirty plates etc from their left.

How to Excel at Garage Sales

Without a doubt, garage sales and the kitchen/garden go hand in hand. If you want to save some big money on household equipment, one of my favourite pastimes is to frequent local sales and second-hand shops in search of bargains.

However, in order to maximize your success, this sort of shopping can benefit from some helpful advice. Experience has taught me that there is an unspoken etiquette when it comes to these affairs and here are my best tips to increase your success:

- Scour through the local newspapers in advance and circle any items which may interest you at Garage Sales, then prioritise and plot your best plan of attack in the time that you have available.

- Always get to Garage Sales a few minutes earlier than the advertised time, even when they ask you not to – EVERYONE does it. If you are late then you are guaranteed slim pickings.

- Garage sales are first in, best dressed so do a quick scout of the wares on offer, and then, if possible, pick up and hold onto any items in which you may be interested – you can always put them back. This sort of tactic works particularly well if you hunt in packs. Possession is nine tenths of the law, so don't let go until you are ready.

- Auctions are a little different as goods need to stay in their place. Make sure, however, that you have a good delve into the boxes so you don't miss any hidden treasures, and don't be afraid to ask the vendor about the history of the items on which you may be bidding.

- Second-hand shops can be a treasure trove of delights and bargains. All manner of kitchen and home-ware items can be found, often for next to nothing. Get to know the staff at the second-hand shop and let them know of any items for which you may be looking. Remember; sometimes it's not what you know, but who you know.

- It's worth remembering that when it comes to second-hand shopping, you win some and you lose some. At the end of the day, don't let the odd dud stop you from cashing in on some excellent bargains. After all, even life doesn't come with a guarantee.

- And lastly, don't be intimidated by those garage sale sharks – they come in all forms and may be heavily disguised as well dressed middle-aged housewives.

A Guide to Box Gardening

THE BENEFITS OF A SIMPLE GARDEN

I really wanted to add this to the first book but I ran out of room. However, I cannot continue without saying that this will be one of the most rewarding, cost saving and worthwhile things you can do for yourself – not to mention the obvious health benefits. It is truly a great stress reducer as well as having obvious fitness and health benefits.

Since book one, I have become a very small part of a national cooking and gardening program. This experience has enabled me to witness first-hand the joys of taking produce from the ground to the table and the delight in teaching kids to cook.

I spent the first 25 years of my marriage believing that gardening was too hard and too time consuming and I used every other excuse under the sun to not get my hands dirty. I completely underestimated the satisfaction and pride I experienced when I harvested my first lettuces (which, I might add, are practically Dumb A*se proof to grow) and the pleasure of turning the week's produce into a delicious and healthy meal. No matter if you have a whole block, or nothing more than a box – anyone can succeed.

And, if you think you can use the excuse that you have no space to grow anything, then I challenge you to make yourself a simple and inexpensive box garden. This can be constructed for less than the cost of a takeaway meal and can easily be made out of recycled materials such as foam boxes.

This photo shows how the same technique can be used on a much larger scale.

The same process applies whether you are using a small foam box as I am showing you on page 11, or building a large scale hot house gardening bed. When using a small box however, you have the added advantage of being able to move the box around according to the sun and weather conditions, or indeed have it indoors near a sunny window.

I first discovered this technique when our garden coordinator Sue started making them with the children at school. The advantages were endless and included the fact that they take up little space, are completely moveable (which is handy if you need someone to baby-sit your veggies while you are away) need watering a lot less often and grow some really awesome stuff.

I am going to share with you this technique which I have used at home with fantastic results.

This style of gardening reduces evaporation and the need for constant watering as the plants draw the moisture up from a 'bath' in the bottom rather than competing with the sun to suck it down. This dramatically increases the time between watering and improves the plants' root development. It is not unusual for plants to go 2-3 weeks between watering in the cooler weather, even longer for bigger beds.

Note: If you are constructing a large scale garden bed where you need to line the 'bath' with thick plastic, it is a good idea to add some sand or old carpet underneath to stop the weight of the water and soil puncturing holes on any stones etc that may be lurking under your base. Having a water-tight base is critical to the whole system. It is also very important that your base is level to allow for even water coverage.

One thing to note is that small seedlings still need some above ground watering for the first week or two until they begin to establish their new root system. Then they are strong enough to dig deep to the water down below.

To get started, I would recommend growing things like herbs, lettuces, radishes, spinach and other common, quick growing greens. I challenge you to try planting a few common plants in such a box and see if that exercise doesn't set you off on a journey into the world of gardening.

What are you waiting for?

EQUIPMENT NEEDED:

1. **A foam fruit/veggie box** with no holes in the bottom (or you can use any water proof vessel in which you can drill an overflow hole).

2. **A piece of PVC pipe**, approximately 5 cm in diameter and 60-70 cm in length (which acts as a water inspection hole). Though this is not an essential step I find it very handy to just peer down the pipe to see if I need to bother getting the hose or not.

3. **A piece of agricultural hose**, approximately 1.2 metres long (a black hose which has small holes and slits in it – available at hardware or rural suppliers).

4. **A small 'elbow' irrigation fitting** which acts as an overflow pipe.

5. **A few rocks** or bits of broken bricks.

6. **An old sock** or something to shove in the end of the pipe to stop the water from gushing through too quickly.

7. **Some hay** or other good drainage material.

8. **A bag of good quality potting mix.**

9. **Seedlings or plants** of your choice.

PUTTING IT TOGETHER

1. Cut a piece of PVC pipe approximately 5 cm in diameter to a length about half as high again as your box. Stand this in one corner of your box.

2. Cut a piece of agricultural drainage pipe long enough to weave over the bottom of the box and then poke it up the side until it is just higher than the top. Shove an old sock in the end (or find some other way of blocking it off) to stop the water from simply gushing out through the end that is in the bottom of the box.

3. Scatter a few rocks over the bottom of the box.

4. Use the elbow fitting to pierce a small hole in the side of the box between a quarter and a third of the way up from the bottom. This will be the overflow point. Make sure you remove any pieces of foam from inside the fitting afterwards or the water won't be able to drain out.

5. Add a layer of straw or other drainage material.

6. Fill the box with a good quality potting soil. This stage represents a great opportunity for your cat to get in there and do its business, so beware!

7. Add a selection of your favourite plants – in this case I have used strawberries. It is a good idea to place some mulch on the top as well.

8. Place your garden hose down into the black agricultural pipe and add water until it begins to seep out of the overflow pipe.

9. Now simply keep an eye on your water level from time to time by looking down the PVC pipe and water when necessary. Don't forget that your plants will also enjoy the benefits of some appropriate fertilizer now and again.

STEPS 1, 2 and 3

STEP 4

STEP 5

STEP 6

STEP 7

STEPS 8 and 9

Indoor Seed Propagation

If you want to take things to the next level, why don't you have a go at raising your own seedlings from scratch? It is much cheaper than buying already established plants, not to mention very satisfying watching nature do its thing right in front of your eyes.

1. Have some sort of waterproof tray in which to sit your punnets.

2. Fill your punnets with a good quality seed-raising or potting mix.

3. Place seeds directly into the punnets according to the depth directions on the seed packet. You can germinate extras and then space them out when you replant them.

4. Place in a sunny position and mist daily with a cheap atomizer. If I am going away, or if the weather is particularly hot, I sometimes add a centimetre of water to the base tray to allow the plants to absorb the water from the bottom up as well.

5. When your seedlings are well and truly established, place your trays outside in the shade for a day or two to harden them off before transplanting them into your garden bed or box. This helps them get used to the outdoor environment and is less of a shock to them than transplanting them straight into the ground.

Before   *After*

Herbing it Up!

Since the times of Adam and Eve, man has been using Nature's finest to his advantage

Cooking with Fresh Herbs

Now I am going to delight in assuming that you may be using the fresh herbs that you have just picked from your own garden boxes.

If not, then pick yourself up some of these little packets of gold from your local market or grocer. They are packed with super good things for you.

Glossary of Herbs

Firstly, it helps to understand the life span of some of the common garden herbs.

Annual plants last for one season only and then die, often setting seeds.
Perennial plants live for at least two years and grow from the same root and stem.
Evergreen plants have leaves that are green, year in year out.

BASIL – Sweet Basil (Annual) has a large bright green leaf and a white flower and usually dies down, whilst Thai Basil (Perennial) has a purple flower and narrower leaves. Basil is delicious with tomato-based dishes and also great with fish, cheese, and in pesto and Thai dishes. There are countless varieties that you can grow.

BAY – (Evergreen) adds great flavour to stocks, stews, fish, marinades, soups etc but always remember to remove the leaves after cooking, as they are for flavour only and not to be eaten. It is one of the few herbs that are better used when dried rather than fresh.

CHIVES – (Perennial) are best used fresh and are delicious added towards the end of soups, salads, chicken, potato and egg dishes. Mix some finely chopped fresh chives with some butter for a tasty spread. Simply snip them off and let them re-grow.

Glossary of Herbs...

CORIANDER – (is an Annual) and from my experience you either love or hate Coriander. It has a softer leaf and looks similar to parsley but has a very distinct flavour and smell. Seeds are also used in cooking.

DILL – (Annual) a feathery type herb with a slight aniseed taste. Leaves and seeds can be used in cooking. Dill is particularly good in egg, seafood and fish dishes.

KAFFIR LIME – I don't think that this is actually a herb but I am going to list it here anyway and it is definitely an Evergreen. The tree resembles that of a lemon or lime but you need to be wary of its thorns. Kaffir lime leaves are traditionally used in Asian cooking, usually in conjunction with galangal (a relation to ginger). The rind (or zest) of the fruit is also commonly used in cooking.

LEMONGRASS – (Perennial/Evergreen) has sharp, reed-like leaves which hold a wonderful citrus flavour. It is a common ingredient in most Asian cooking. The roots can also be used, along with the lower white part of the stem. Discard the long outer green leaves.

MINT – (Perennial) comes in many different flavours and is exceptionally good with lamb, potatoes, in salads and chocolate or lemon based desserts and drinks.

OREGANO – (also known as marjoram, is a Perennial) It is a common herb in Italian, Greek and Mexican cooking and goes well with all kinds of meat.

Glossary of Herbs...

PARSLEY – (Annual but drops seeds and you will have it forever) comes in different varieties and goes really well with egg, potato, pasta and salad dishes as well as with most meats.

ROSEMARY – (A woody Evergreen shrub) – once you have it, you've got it for life as it is very hardy. It is one of my favourite herbs and is terrific with lamb, potato, fish, vegetables and in soups etc. etc. It can be a bit stick-like so it is best to strip the leaves and chop very finely or crush in a mortar and pestle. Alternatively remove the whole sprigs after cooking.

SAGE – (Evergreen) has long, greenish grey bumpy leaves. It is particularly good with meats such as lamb, pork and sausages but should be used sparingly. Sage tea is great for a sore throat with some honey and boiling water.

TARRAGON – (Perennial) Also known as French Tarragon, it has a liquorice type flavour and is delicious with fish, eggs, chicken and vegetables. It is an essential part of French cooking but should be used sparingly as it can overpower a dish.

THYME – (Perennial) has a subtle lemony mint taste and does well in the warmer months. It is a common accompaniment to meat, fish, chicken, eggs and potatoes and is commonly used in stuffing and seasonings. It is also an important herb in French cooking.

Fresh Herb Pesto (GF)

Serve it with your favourite crackers or crusty bread (or other gluten free option). To make Basil Pesto simply replace the parsley and chervil with basil. This pesto is also delicious tossed through some freshly cooked fettuccine pasta with a good drizzle of extra virgin olive oil.

INGREDIENTS:

- ½ cup of tightly packed fresh parsley
- ½ cup of tightly packed fresh chervil (A relative of parsley with a slightly aniseed flavour. If you can't grow or find chervil, simply replace it with more parsley.)
- 1 cup of toasted walnuts (or pine nuts)
- 1 clove of garlic, peeled and crushed
- The juice and zest of half a lemon
- ½ cup of grated Parmesan cheese
- ¾ cup of olive oil

METHOD:

1. Place the walnuts in a small frying pan over a medium heat. No oil is necessary. Toast until fragrant, rolling the pan around to avoid burning. Remove.
2. Place all pesto ingredients (except for oil) in the food processor and pulse a couple of times.
3. Leave the processor running and add the oil gradually by pouring into the opening at the top of your machine.
4. Serve with your choice of accompaniments.

Chargrilled Vegetables in Herb Oil (GF)

Keep this oil indefinitely in your fridge so it will be ready to use in your favourite recipes. I like to douse things like fresh eggplant, capsicum, sweet potatoes, zucchini and sometimes tomatoes before placing them in a hot pan or on the BBQ hot plate. Also great with steak but make sure you let the flavours develop before using.

INGREDIENTS:

- 2 cups of extra virgin olive oil
- 2 cloves of garlic, peeled and crushed
- 2 teaspoons of stripped and finely chopped rosemary (no jokes please)
- 2 teaspoons of stripped and finely chopped basil
- 1 teaspoon of stripped and finely chopped thyme
- ½ finely diced red spur chilli
- Vegetables of your choice, sliced evenly to chargrill.

Herbing it Up!

Fresh Zucchini and Spinach Soup with Coriander (GF)

Don't let this rather bland looking soup put you off trying this recipe, as some have hailed it the best soup they have ever eaten.

INGREDIENTS:

- 1-2 tablespoons of vegetable oil for frying
- 2 large potatoes, peeled, washed and roughly chopped
- 1 onion, peeled and roughly chopped
- 2 cloves of garlic, peeled and diced
- 3 large fresh spinach or silver beet leaves, white stems removed and shredded
- 1 garden zucchini, washed and roughly chopped (removing any seeds and the tough centre section leaving you with 500 grams of good flesh)
- 5 gluten free vegetable or chicken stock cubes, crumbled
- 7 cups of water
- The juice of ½ a lemon
- Some freshly chopped coriander to serve, (this can be optional)
- Salt and pepper to taste

METHOD:

1. Heat the oil to a medium heat and sauté the onions and garlic until the onion begins to turn golden.
2. Add the roughly chopped zucchini and potatoes and continue to stir for another minute or so, adding a splash of extra water to the saucepan if it looks too dry or starts to stick to the pan.
3. Add the water and crumbled stock cubes, then increase the heat and bring to the boil.
4. Reduce the heat and simmer for 20 minutes or until the vegetables are tender.
5. Turn off the heat and stir in the lemon juice and shredded spinach.
6. Allow to cool for a few minutes and then carefully purée with a hand blender before garnishing with the fresh coriander.

Easy Egg Frittata with Fresh Herbs (GF)

When I was young I used to come home from a big night out and cook up my own version of this to appease my munchies. It's cheap, filling and delicious.

INGREDIENTS:

- 1 brown onion, peeled and diced
- 2 medium potatoes, peeled and diced
- 1 small sweet potato (or piece of pumpkin) peeled and thinly sliced or diced
- ½ large red capsicum, diced
- 2-3 large spinach or silver beet leaves, washed, white stems removed and shredded
- A small quantity of gluten free meat, eg bacon, chicken, chorizo etc
- A good handful of fresh herbs such as dill, rosemary, oregano, parsley etc, finely shredded. You could substitute with a good teaspoon of dried Italian herbs.
- 6-8 eggs, whisked
- ¾ - 1 cup of reduced fat milk
- ½ cup of reduced fat grated cheese
- Salt and freshly ground black pepper
- 1 tablespoon of oil for frying

Note: I will sometimes add some leftover cooked pasta as well, though obviously this would have to be a gluten free variety.

METHOD:

1. Heat oil in a large non-stick frying pan over a MEDIUM heat.
2. Add diced onion, potatoes, (and pumpkin if using) capsicum and meat of your choice. Fry until vegetables are tender and have caramelised (turned golden) stirring often to avoid sticking. If vegetables do begin to stick, add another teaspoon of oil and loosen the bottom with wooden spoon.
3. Whisk the eggs and milk together in a jug with the salt and pepper and then stir in the cheese, fresh herbs and shredded spinach.
4. Make sure vegetables in the pan are arranged evenly and then gently pour the egg mixture over the top. Reduce the heat to LOW and place the lid on the frying pan.
5. Cook gently until the egg is set on top. If you smell it start to burn, turn the heat down immediately.
6. At this point you have a few choices:

1) If you don't want the top golden, it is ready to gently cut and serve
2) You can cut it into sections and gently turn it over to brown on the other side, or
3) If your frying pan has an oven proof handle, you can slip it under the griller to brown slightly on top before serving.

Herbing it Up! 19

Mustard Herb Pilaf (GF)

What is a 'pilaf' you ask? Pilaf is a rice dish which has been steamed in a broth - or in this case chicken stock. I will forewarn you now that this dish takes both time and attention (a bit like risotto) but you will be rewarded ten-fold with the sensational and irresistible taste. This pilaf will take a good 40 minutes to prepare but OMG - you will not be able to stop eating it and you may just turn Vegetarian in the process. It is delicious hot or cold, on its own, or with your favourite cut of meat. Enjoy!

INGREDIENTS:

- Approximately 2 tablespoons of butter (the flavour is much better than margarine)
- 1 onion, peeled, halved and thinly sliced
- 1½ cups of dry white rice
- 2 gluten free chicken stock cubes, crumbled (I use stock cubes that each make 500 ml of stock when water is added, so read your stock cube directions)
- Approximately 750 ml of boiling water, maybe more
- 1 dessertspoon of honey
- 1 dessertspoon of seeded mustard (or 1 teaspoon of dry mustard powder for the gluten free guest unless your paste is safe)
- A good (and I mean big) handful of fresh herbs and greens, washed and roughly chopped. These could include finely chopped rosemary, chopped oregano, parsley or shredded spinach etc
- Salt and pepper

METHOD:

1. Boil your electric kettle and then dissolve the crumbled stock cubes in a heatproof jug with the 750 ml of boiling water. Stir in the honey and set aside.
2. Melt the butter in a medium saucepan and add the onion. Fry until the onion begins to turn clear and has a nice golden appearance.
3. Add the dry rice and stir around the pan for a good 2-3 minutes until the rice has taken on all the pan flavours and some colour.
4. Begin adding the chicken stock, about a quarter of a cup at a time. Stir often and don't add more stock until the previous lot has been absorbed. This is the time-consuming process as you can't afford to leave the saucepan in case the rice begins to burn. Time to grab your favourite book and sit near the saucepan.
5. While this is happening, wash and roughly chop your herbs and greens.
6. Continue adding the stock to the rice gradually for probably the next twenty minutes or so, until the rice is soft when you bite it. This is the irresistible part when you just want to keep eating it.
7. Stir in the seeded mustard, herbs, greens, salt and pepper.
8. Turn off the heat and remove to the side. Place the lid on the saucepan and let it sit. Check after a few minutes and if you think the rice is a little dry, then add a small amount of extra boiling water and stir, replacing the lid.
9. Serves 2 as a main or 4 as a side dish.

Couscous Tabouli with Fresh Parsley

Tabouli is traditionally made with burghul (cracked wheat) though this is sometimes hard to find in smaller shops. Couscous is much more readily available and faster to prepare.

INGREDIENTS:

- 3 cups of cooked couscous (follow directions on packet – it's easy)
- ¼ cup of olive oil
- Juice of 1 large lemon
- 1 Lebanese cucumber, unpeeled and diced
- 2 spring onions, finely sliced
- 1 large tomato, diced (or use some halved cherry tomatoes)
- 3-4 cups of fresh parsley, tightly packed
- Salt and pepper to taste

METHOD:

1. Place the parsley in your food processor and pulse for 2-3 seconds. Alternatively you can just chop it finely.
2. Combine all ingredients in a large bowl and stir lightly.

Rustic Potato Salad with Rosemary (GF)

This is a delicious potato salad with a low fat dressing. The rosemary can be replaced with coriander if you prefer.

INGREDIENTS:

- 4-5 large potatoes, well washed, imperfections removed and skins left on
- 1 sweet potato (kumara) skin on but washed well
- The juice and zest of a lemon
- ½ a red spur chilli, finely diced to disperse the heat (Do not touch your eyes or privates when chopping chilli!)
- A couple of tablespoons of finely chopped rosemary or coriander (remove the woody stalks from the rosemary)
- Desired amount of natural yogurt to combine
- Some finely diced red onion, optional
- Freshly ground salt and black pepper

METHOD:

1. Prick the washed potatoes several times with a fork and then place evenly around the microwave tray. Cook them on HIGH until soft. Alternatively you could cook them on the racks of your preheated 180°C oven for 30-40 minutes until soft and golden. If you do this, then proceed to step 4.
2. Preheat your griller.
3. Grill the potatoes for a few minutes on each side until their skins are crispy and golden. This adds extra tastiness to the salad. Remove and cool.
4. Cut the potatoes to the desired shape and size.
5. Stir in the lemon juice, zest, chilli, rosemary, yogurt and salt and pepper. Serve.

How to Masta Pasta

These easy tips will have you on your way to a pasta making addiction
WARNING: May be detrimental to the thighs

Making your own Pasta – OMG!

How much fun is this? When I borrowed someone's machine and made pasta for the first time I knew that I was heading for an addiction! That craving took me straight to the shop to get my very own pasta machine and stock up on 00 flour.

You can make pasta using just ordinary Plain flour (I would just knead it that extra bit more) but specialty pasta flours produce better results. Nonetheless I was pretty happy with my first attempt. You can pick up a cheap pasta machine for as little as $30, so stick one on your Chrissy list.

Choosing the correct pasta for the job can no doubt be daunting to the novice, but really, unless you are buying coloured pasta which has had a flavour added to it, they pretty much all taste the same. Some people say that thicker sauces (containing meat or cream) should have thinner pasta with them such as Spaghetti Bolognaise, and the other way around for thinner sauces. Personally I don't think it matters that much.

These are a few of the more common pastas that you can have a go at making or find on the supermarket shelf if you are not that way inclined.

- **Spaghetti** – is long, thin and is solid in the middle – often served with meat or cream based sauces (easy to make)
- **Tubular** – comes in various length and sizes and is hollow in the middle – commonly used in soups, casseroles or heavier dishes
- **Fettuccine** – is a form of ribbon pasta that is long, thin and flat – used with lighter sauces (easy to make)
- **Rotini** – is a spiral shaped pasta – common in salads and casseroles
- **Lasagne** – (easy to make) is long, wide, flat sheets – used for making lasagna (and ravioli and tortellini if making it fresh)

Basic Pasta Making

BASIC PASTA DOUGH RECIPE:

- For every 100 grams of '00' fine Italian Plain flour (or other 'strong' Plain flour)
- You use 1 egg

A teaspoon or so of water, or a little more flour may be needed as all eggs vary in their weight. Adjust these as you are making it.

As a rule you will need 100 grams of flour per hungry adult if making spaghetti or fettuccine. This will be plenty – less for kids.

FOOD PROCESSOR METHOD:

1. Place the required amount of flour in the food processor bowl.
2. Whisk the egg/s well with a fork in a small jug.
3. Set the processor going on a medium speed and drizzle in the whisked egg/s. The mixture should come together in a ball around the blade. If it has not come together, add a teaspoon of water with the machine running, or if it seems too wet, a teaspoon more of flour. More of either may be necessary.
4. Remove from the processor onto a very lightly floured board, as you don't want to dry the dough out with too much extra flour.
5. Knead lightly for a couple of minutes until the dough becomes smooth and elastic. If at any time you think it is too dry, simply lightly wet your hands and continue. Alternatively if it seems too sticky, put a little extra flour on your hands.
6. When it's a nice elastic consistency, wrap very well in plastic wrap and leave for at least 20 minutes to 'rest' before putting through the machine. For pasta making this means time for the pasta dough to get the gluten developing and NOT that you are feeling sleepy! Refrigerate if in a warm environment.

Note: My sister-in-law uses the plastic blade on her food processor and processes it for a bit longer. She tells me this means she doesn't need to knead it. It would be worth a try. At the end of the day, you just need your dough to be elastic and have the ability to spring back. Then, into the fridge for a 'rest'.

PASTA DOUGH BY HAND METHOD:

1. Make a volcano type arrangement with the flour on a clean bench.
2. Now pretend your egg is the lava and crack it into the middle of the flour.
3. Use your fingertips in a circular motion to gradually incorporate the egg into the flour and as with the method above add more water or flour if required. Hand-made pasta needs more kneading – most likely up to 10 minutes to get to the same elastic consistency.
4. When nice and elastic, wrap in plastic wrap for at least 20 minutes – refrigerate if in a warm environment.

ROLLING THE DOUGH WITH A PASTA MACHINE:

1. Divide dough if necessary so you are working with pieces about the size of a small apple.

2. Shape dough into a long sausage shape and flatten evenly with your hands. Some people like to use a rolling pin to get the basic long, thin shape.

3. Sprinkle some extra flour over the rollers of the pasta machine.

4. Begin with the machine on its fattest setting (usually number '1' but some machines work the opposite way). Feed it through the machine with one hand whilst turning the handle (which is in the roller hole) with the other – or get your mate to help you.

5. If necessary brush a little extra flour over both sides of the sheet of pasta before folding it into thirds, bringing the short sides of the rectangle into the centre. Now turn 45 degrees and run it through on setting '1' again.

6. Repeat twice more. This folding and turning really gets the gluten working in the dough.

7. Proceed to thickness 2 on the dial and continue to run the pasta through once at each number, sprinkling the machine and/or pasta with more flour when necessary. It may be necessary to cut your sheets into shorter pieces if they get too long.

8. When your pasta is at the desired thickness, you're done and ready to make either lasagne or ravioli. After putting it through at about number 6 or 7, if making spaghetti or fettuccine, move your handle and run the dough through the preferred cutting attachment.

9. Leave your pasta to either hang over a rack (some people use a clothes airer) or dry slightly on a floured bench or on a clean tea towel for about 15 minutes before cooking – just long enough to get your salted water boiling.

Note: I have found that on some occasions the pasta has not cut through properly when making spaghetti or fettuccine. This has usually been because the dough has been too moist. It usually comes apart when it's cooked in the boiling water but if you are not happy with it, try rolling it up again and repeat the process, this time adding more flour, especially before the final cutting run.

Batches of dough can also be frozen for later use if need be or made a day or two ahead and kept well wrapped in the fridge.

Cooking Fresh Pasta

METHOD:

1. Bring a large pot of salted water to the boil.
2. Drop fresh pasta gently into the water and boil until just cooked. This usually only takes 3-5 minutes for fresh pasta. In the case of ravioli, it floats to the surface when it's ready. Pasta should be 'al dente' which means still with a slight amount of resistance when chewed.
3. Drain and serve immediately with your favourite sauce.

Lemon Cream Fettuccine with Tuna

I can't tell a lie; this is harsh on the hips but totally delicious and very easy. For a lower calorie option, try replacing the cream with low fat ricotta instead.

SAUCE INGREDIENTS:

- 3 large egg yolks
- The juice of 1-2 lemons
- 4 tablespoons of grated Parmesan cheese
- 1½ cups of cream
- Salt and freshly ground black pepper
- 2 small cans of drained lemon pepper tuna (or a large tin of drained tuna with lemon pepper added to it)
- Extra lemon juice if required
- Desired amount of freshly cooked fettuccine

METHOD:

1. Combine the egg yolks, cream and Parmesan cheese in a microwave safe jug and whisk well. Cook on MEDIUM for 1-3 minutes, stirring once. You are trying to get the sauce hot but not let it boil.
2. Stir in the tuna and half the lemon juice.
3. Add the sauce and tuna to the freshly drained, hot pasta and stir well.
4. Season with salt and pepper and add extra lemon juice to taste.

Spinach and Ricotta Ravioli with (Not Quite) Burnt Butter Sage

RAVIOLI INGREDIENTS:

- 1 quantity of ready rolled lasagne style pasta, rolled to a thin setting (200 grams of flour mix will make enough for 2 people)
- 6-8 large spinach leaves, washed and white stems removed
- ½ tub of fresh ricotta cheese
- 1 egg, beaten
- ¼ cup of freshly grated Parmesan cheese
- 1 teaspoon of a heavy cream such as Mascarpone
- 1 rounded teaspoon of Cornflour in ¼ cup of water, for brushing
- Salt and pepper

METHOD:

1. Put a large saucepan of salted water on to boil.
2. Place damp spinach in a microwave safe dish with a lid and cook on HIGH for 1-2 minutes. Cool and drain with paper towel. Chop finely.
3. Combine spinach, ricotta, egg, Parmesan, salt, pepper and cream in a bowl and mix well.
4. Lay your long pasta sheets carefully out on a lightly floured bench.
5. Place small teaspoons of the mixture at 3 cm intervals.
6. Combine the Cornflour and water and use a brush (or your finger) to paint around the edges of the mixture. Do this quickly so it doesn't dry out.
7. Carefully lay another sheet of pasta on top and then press down firmly around the filling. You don't want any bits left open or the water will get in.
8. Cut into squares or circles using either a ravioli cutter, knife or biscuit cutter. Ensure edges are well sealed.
9. Drop ravioli into rapidly boiling salted water and cook for 2-3 minutes until it floats to the surface.
10. Drain and serve with the (Not Quite) Burnt Butter Sage recipe following.

(Not Quite) Burnt Butter Sage

Now don't take the burnt butter part literally because any DA cook would realise that butter that was actually burnt wouldn't taste too good.

INGREDIENTS:

- 2-3 big tablespoons of good quality butter
- A generous handful of fresh sage leaves which have been washed and stripped from their stalks
- A pinch of nutmeg, optional

METHOD:

1. Melt the butter in a small frying pan and throw in the sage leaves.
2. Stir continually until butter turns golden (not burnt) and your sage leaves are crispy. Add more butter if desired.
3. Add a pinch of nutmeg before pouring over your ravioli and serving.

Chook's Seafood Marinara

My mate Chook is an excellent cook and makes a mean Seafood Marinara.

INGREDIENTS:

- Approximately 500 grams (or desired amount) of seafood marinara mix or fresh seafood of your choice
- 2 cloves of garlic, peeled and crushed
- 1 x 400 gram can of diced tomatoes (or 5 whole chopped)
- 1 tablespoon of tomato paste
- ½ cup of last night's leftover dry white wine
- Some freshly chopped parsley
- Freshly ground salt and pepper
- Juice of half a lemon
- 1 tablespoon of oil
- Desired amount of freshly cooked spaghetti or fettuccine

METHOD:

1. Heat the oil in a large, heavy based saucepan.
2. Fry the garlic for 1-2 minutes over a medium heat.
3. Add the tomatoes and tomato paste and continue to cook for another couple of minutes. Raw tomatoes will take a little longer of course. You may use your potato masher at this point to break them up a little or else purée them.
4. Add the wine and cook until slightly reduced (thickened).
5. Add the seafood and simmer for a further 5-8 minutes or until the seafood is cooked through.
6. Add salt and pepper to taste.
7. Pour over your freshly cooked spaghetti or fettuccine. Finish with the lemon juice and chopped parsley.

How to Masta Pasta

Roasted Pumpkin and Spinach Lasagne

This vegetarian dish is the perfect way to show off your new pasta making skills and if you simply can't live without meat, try adding a little cooked, shredded chicken between the layers. Be aware that fresh pasta will cook much quicker than the commercially bought sheets, so increase your cooking time for those. The rich flavours of the roasted vegetables in this recipe will go perfectly with a simple green salad.

INGREDIENTS:

- Some freshly made lasagne sheets (300 gram flour mixture should be plenty)
- Approximately 700 grams of butternut pumpkin, peeled and cut into chunks
- 1 large red capsicum, deseeded and cut into quarters
- 4 cloves of garlic, peeled and left whole
- 1 large brown onion, peeled and quartered
- Some olive oil for roasting
- Salt and pepper
- 1 bunch of spinach leaves, washed and white stems removed
- Approximately ⅔ cup of cream
- Some grated cheese

METHOD:

- Preheat the oven to 180°C.
- Place the pumpkin, capsicum, garlic and onion in a baking dish and drizzle with olive oil, salt and pepper. Roast uncovered in the oven until the vegetables are nice and golden, stirring occasionally. I will sometimes pre-cook my vegetables in the microwave to speed up their roasting time. Remove and cool a little, but leave the oven on.
- Place the roasted vegetables and half of the cream into your food processor bowl and pulse the mixture a couple of times.
- Place your prepared spinach into a microwave safe dish and cook on HIGH for 1 minute or until just wilted.
- Grease a 25 cm square baking dish. If you are not using fresh pasta, place 2 teaspoons of water in the bottom.
- Begin making multiple layers of pasta, pumpkin spread and wilted spinach. Finish with the pumpkin spread, the remaining cream and some grated cheese on top.
- Cover with foil (shiny side down) and bake for 20-25 minutes. Remove the foil and cook for a further 5 minutes. Serves 4-6.

Bread Making for Beginners

Venturing from the shearing shed to the kitchen

Basic Guides and Tips

Once you know how to make basic bread dough you can adapt it to lots of other things such as pizza bases, pides (flat breads), hot cross buns, bread rolls etc. Our local bread-making expert, Helen kindly shared her family's recipe with me as it was much faster than my own. This makes it perfect for the DA cook.

- Keep yeast sachets in the fridge to prolong their life. Once opened, store the yeast in an airtight jar or container as the life and effectiveness of yeast is limited once opened.
- Dough can be frozen in portion sizes to use at a later date by wrapping in plastic wrap or in a freezer bag. Always defrost slowly at room temperature.
- It always pays to spray your plastic wrap with a bit of cooking oil prior to covering your dough, otherwise it will tend to stick as it rises and makes contact. I have made this mistake more than once. Other people like to use a clean tea towel instead or simply just let it sit.
- Don't underestimate the interior of your car as the perfect warm spot for rising dough.
- Bread will take approximately 45 minutes to cook in a 180°C oven (it should sound hollow when you tap the top with your knuckles).
- Bread sticks, pides and rolls will take approximately 20 minutes.
- Pizzas around 8-10 minutes, or until golden.

Basic Bread Dough

The recipe makes 4 medium loaves of bread, 8 pizza bases, 4 large bread sticks, 20 large bread rolls or 4 pides – all of course dependent on their sizes. This is a basic recipe which can be tweaked anyway you like - often only half a batch is required.

INGREDIENTS:

- 6 cups of Bread Flour (this specialty flour can be bought as different varieties eg multigrain, whole meal, soy and linseed, rye etc)
- 1 rounded tablespoon (8 gram sachet) of dry yeast
- 1 tablespoon of Bread Improver (if using premix bread flour this is not necessary)
- 2 teaspoons of fine salt (if using premix bread flour this is not necessary)
- 3 cups of hot water (not boiling)
- 1 tablespoon of oil

METHOD:

1. Place the dry ingredients in a bowl and make a 'well' in the centre.
2. Pour in both the hot water and oil and mix until combined.
3. Tip out onto a well-oiled (or floured) bench and knead for 10 minutes. Sometimes I find I might need to add a little extra flour if I think it is too sticky. If you have a machine with a dough hook you can use that to do the mixing, otherwise you will be building up your muscles.
4. When finished kneading, shape and place on your tray or in your bread tins and leave in a warm, draught free place to rise until they are about double in size – about 45 minutes. Then, for a nice golden look, brush with a beaten egg and water wash and sprinkle with some sesame or poppy seeds and cook for the required amount of time – see above.

Basic Pide Bread

- ¼ of the Basic Bread Dough (see previous recipe)

EGG WASH:

- 1 small egg, lightly whisked
- 1 tablespoon of water
- Some sesame seeds for sprinkling

PIDE METHOD:

1. Shape the dough into a long pide, flattening to approx 1½ cm thick with your hands. Place on a biscuit tray lined with baking paper and cover with a clean tea towel. Allow to sit and rise in a warm, draught free place until almost double in size. 'Draught' does not refer to beer even though it is a yeast product!
2. Preheat the oven to 200°C.
3. Brush the pide with the egg and water wash and make several trenches diagonally across the top, using your finger or the handle of a wooden spoon. Sprinkle with sesame seeds and bake in a hot oven for 15-20 minutes or until cooked through.

Turkish Pizza Pide

This is an absolute winner and can be solely vegetarian or have meat added. Of course you can buy a ready-made pide, or have a go at making your own if you have time (see instructions). Note that the dough can be made a day ahead and kept in the refrigerator, just make sure you remove it from the fridge at least 2 hours before you are ready to cook it. This pide recipe makes enough to feed 8 people for a hearty snack or 4 people for a solid meal.

INGREDIENTS:

- 1 cooked Turkish pide loaf, or similar long flat bread (preferably grainy or whole meal)
- 2-3 tablespoons of your favourite chutney or BBQ sauce
- Approximately 2 cups of peeled and roughly diced pumpkin
- 2 cloves of garlic, peeled and roughly chopped
- 1 medium sweet potato, peeled and roughly diced
- 1 red or brown onion, peeled, cut in half and finely sliced
- 3 - 4 good sized silver beet or spinach leaves
- 1 small red capsicum, cut into strips
- 1 small jalapeño chilli (for an optional hit – use gloves if necessary)
- A handful of cooked and shredded chicken, optional
- Approximately half a block of feta cheese, crumbled
- ½ cup of grated cheese
- 1-3 tablespoons of oil or butter for frying, more if needed
- Salt and freshly ground black pepper
- Fresh basil leaves for serving, optional

Bread Making for Beginners

METHOD:

1. Preheat the oven to 180°C and line a biscuit tray with baking paper.
2. Prepare all of your ingredients as above.
3. Heat oil in a large frying pan and add the onion, sweet potato, garlic, pumpkin, capsicum and jalapeño (if using). Fry until the vegetables are tender and have begun to caramelise and turn golden. Add more butter or oil if the pan becomes dry. This will take approximately 15–20 minutes. Remove from heat. To save some time, the vegetables could be pre-cooked in the microwave for a few minutes first before browning up in the pan. This pizza could also be made with leftover roasted vegetables.
4. Wash the silver beet leaves under running water, shake dry, cut out white stems and finely shred. Add the shredded spinach to the other vegetables, lightly stir and then turn off the heat and allow it to wilt.
5. Cut the pide in halves horizontally to open up. For best results, spray with a little cooking oil and place it in the hot oven for 3-4 minutes to develop a toasty crust. Remove and spread the chutney evenly over both pieces.
6. Cover both pieces of the bread with the vegetable mixture.
7. Scatter the shredded chicken and feta over the pides and finish with a small amount of grated cheese, salt and pepper.
8. Bake (or grill) for around 12-15 minutes or until golden. Garnish with fresh basil if desired.

Plaited Bread Sticks

You do the same with the dough as you would with your hair.

INGREDIENTS:

- Desired quantity of the basic bread recipe dough
- Beaten egg and water wash
- Poppy or sesame seeds

METHOD:

1. Preheat the oven to 180°C.
2. Shape your dough into a long, thin sausage shape. Lay onto your tray lined with baking paper. Alternatively you can buy special French stick tins in which case you would need to perform step 3 before laying them in the tins.
3. Make three long cuts in each piece of dough, almost to the ends, and then carefully plait them. To plait you continuously bring the outside piece to the centre i.e. left piece to the centre, right piece to the centre, left piece…..and so on.
4. Cover the dough with a clean tea towel and sit to rise in a warm, draught free place until doubled in size.
5. Brush with the egg and water wash, and sprinkle with seeds before baking.

Pear and Pancetta Pizza with Walnuts and Honey

This might sound an odd combination, but trust me, it's delicious – I even had children make this for the Premier of South Australia.

A famous Australian Chef once told me that loading pizzas with cheese is unnecessary, detracts from the other flavours and is not that good for your waistline! I am now converted forever. She also told me how to get a nice crispy base by placing the dough on a hot tray and pre-baking it for a couple of minutes before removing and adding your toppings. Of course this is not necessary for a delicious pizza, but it is something with which you can experiment.

INGREDIENTS:

- 1 large pizza base (or a ball of fresh bread dough about the size of a large orange -see Basic Bread Dough recipe – ¼ mixture)
- 2 tablespoons of cream
- 2 small pears, peeled and thinly sliced
- 4-5 rashers of pancetta, (or prosciutto or bacon) roughly torn
- A small handful of walnuts, roughly chopped
- A very small amount of cheese, optional (try breaking up leftover Camembert or some blue cheese if you are a fan)
- A drizzle of warm honey for serving
- Some fresh basil leaves for serving

METHOD:

1. Preheat the oven to 200ºC.
2. Grease a large pizza tray and place into the oven to get hot. This is if you want a crisp base, otherwise leave it cold.
3. Make sure you have all ingredients prepared and ready to go as time is critical if you want that crispy base.
4. Gently roll out your dough and then transfer it straight onto your hot, well-greased pizza tray. Place into the oven for 2 minutes then remove to a heat proof surface.
5. Quickly smear the base with the cream, arrange the sliced pears, pancetta, cheese and walnuts and return to the hot oven for 8-10 minutes, or until cooked.
6. Meanwhile, warm a small amount of honey (about 2 dessertspoons) in a cup in the microwave.
7. Drizzle the cooked pizza with warm honey and sprinkle on the freshly torn basil leaves just before serving.

Hot Cross Buns

Bring out your artistic flair by getting into the spirit of Easter and making your own Hot Cross Buns.

- 6 cups of white bread flour
- 1 tablespoon of bread improver (if not using premix flour)
- 1 rounded tablespoon of dry yeast (8 gram sachet)
- 2 cups of mixed dried fruit of your choice (I use currants and sultanas)
- 1 tablespoon of mixed spice
- 1 cup of dry powdered milk
- 1 cup of sugar
- 3 cups of very hot water
- 1 tablespoon of oil

GLAZE:

- 2 dessertspoons of sugar dissolved in:
- ¼ cup of boiling water

FLOUR PASTE CROSSES:

- 1 cup of Plain flour mixed to a fairly thick, smooth paste with:
- 10 tablespoons of water – add more if necessary

METHOD:

1. Mix all the dry bun ingredients and then add the water and oil.
2. Knead and shape into buns, remembering that they will almost double in size when risen. Putting them close together on the tray can give you those nice square sides like the bought ones.
3. Cover and rise in a warm, draught free place until doubled in size – usually around 45 minutes. As I mentioned previously the front seat of your car is an ideal place on a warm day!
4. Preheat the oven to 180°C.
5. Place the flour paste into a cake icing gun or use a plastic freezer bag with a small hole in one corner to squeeze out the mixture. Mark buns with crosses and cook for approximately 20 minutes.
6. Remove buns from the oven and then baste with the glaze while still warm. The full recipe will make approximately 36 medium hot cross buns.

36 Bread Making for Beginners

Seafood Made Simple

Everything you need to know to take it from the ocean to the kitchen table - including the odd safety tip

From the Ocean to the Table

There is nothing that can compare with the feeling of catching your own produce, straight from Australia's deep, blue sea. And the taste is second to none. Therefore I want to dedicate a chunk of this book to encouraging you to venture off your couch and into perhaps a foreign zone that really fits under the 'Hunting and Gathering' category.

Here we will examine some basic cleaning techniques for many common varieties of seafood, and then show you how to prepare them for cooking. I realise that many of you will already know how to do some of this, but this section is primarily dedicated to those of you who may be attempting this for the first time.

Each variety of seafood has its own specific requirements and techniques for catching, and this can be limitless. There are 1001 books and a whole Internet full of information on fishing that you can source, so I'm not going there.

As to where to go for good advice, the best place to start is your local fishing and outdoor store. They will have a good knowledge of your specific area and be able to advise you of suitable tackle, tide times and other relevant information to aid in your success. The rest comes down to practice and luck, of which I wish you all the very best.

Whatever the outcome, you have saved the batteries on your remote control and soaked up a bit of vitamin D for the day. If worse comes to worst, you wouldn't be the first person to stop by the fish shop on the way home!

WARNING: *Be aware of fish limits, sizes and licensing, which differ from State to State. Make sure you know what applies to you and your area as this can be a very expensive mistake if the authorities come to visit.*

How to Fillet a Fish

Here Jae uses our famous King George Whiting as an example.

Note: For best results you will need a very sharp knife with a thin, flexible blade. Head to your local fishing shop where you will find a whole range of suitable knives.

Before you begin, make sure you remove all scales from the fish, either by using a commercially bought hand scaler or the edge of a serrated scaling knife. Better still, if boating, invest in a scaling bag that does all the slimy work for you.

1. Make a cut, just behind the gill, down to the backbone.

2. Now change the angle of your knife to horizontally slice the fillet from the fish. Start from the gill end and move towards the tail, running your knife along the top of the backbone. Aim for one gliding cut if possible, using the backbone as your guide.

3. Turn the fish over and repeat on the other side.

4. Remove the 'belly' bones by making a thin 30 degree slice along the top quarter of the fish (where the belly would have been).

5. Remove the remaining backbones by cutting a small V at the top of the fillet and using your fingers to assess if you have got all the bones out. My pet hate is finding bones in my fish. Now give the fillets a final rinse, preferably in fresh sea water, before cooking or freezing.

Seafood Made Simple

Lemon and Dill Crusted Whiting

This is one of my favourite recipes to prepare for guests. I can have the fish crumbed the day before if need be, and then quickly fried up and draped on top of a lovely green salad for a stunning culinary result.

INGREDIENTS:

- 6 whiting fillets
- 3 slices of stale bread (try using grainy or wholemeal)
- Grated lemon zest of 1-2 lemons
- 3-4 tablespoons of finely chopped fresh dill (or rosemary is also nice)
- Approximately 3 tablespoons of finely grated Parmesan cheese, optional
- A good shake of salt and freshly ground black pepper
- 1 egg, beaten
- ¼ cup of milk
- ½ cup of Plain flour, more if necessary
- Vegetable oil for frying

METHOD:

1. Place bread slices, dill, salt and pepper into your food processor bowl and process until fine. Alternatively you can buy pre-made bread crumbs.
2. Stir in the lemon zest and cheese.
3. Place beaten egg and milk onto a large plate and whisk well with a fork.
4. Place flour on another plate, and crumb mixture on a third.
5. Begin by coating the fish in the flour, followed by egg mixture and finally into the crumb mix. See the original Aussie Dumb A*se Cookbook page 20 for a pictorial guide.
6. Heat oil in a large frying pan over a medium to high heat. Alternatively you could deep-fry them. You will know when the oil is hot enough as a piece of food will sizzle on contact. Don't let it get smoking hot.
7. When hot, fry fish until golden on both sides – approximately 2-3 minutes per side. Continue until all cooked.
8. Remove and drain on paper towel.
9. Serve under a pile of your favourite salad with a dash of seafood sauce.

Snapper Italiane GF

INGREDIENTS:

- 1 snapper or other large fish suitable for baking; scaled, gutted and washed thoroughly
- 1 large jar of gluten free pasta sauce – preferably your own home made stuff
- ½ onion, peeled and thinly sliced
- Sprigs of rosemary, lemon thyme, basil, oregano, dill etc
- A few cherry tomatoes
- 1 lemon, thinly sliced
- Ground salt and black pepper

METHOD:

1. Preheat the oven to 180°C.
2. Place the snapper in a large, greased baking dish.
3. Stuff half the fresh herbs and some of the onion rings inside the cavity of the fish.
4. Pour over the pasta sauce.
5. Lay the lemon slices on top of the fish and throw on the remaining herbs.
6. Scatter the remaining onion on top along with the cherry tomatoes.
7. Cover with foil (shiny side down) and cook for 30-40 minutes or until fish turns white in the thickest part.

Neil's Smoked Snook

If you love your fishing, invest in your own smoke box. There are all manner of sizes and types on the market starting from well under $100. The process and length of time it will take to smoke your fish will depend on which type of smoker you have (hot or cold) and the size of your fish.

Here is a guide to Neil's Smoked Snook using a cheap, commercially bought hot smoker which uses a methylated spirits burner. These are available, along with wood chips of various flavours, at your local fishing or hardware shop.

To prepare the scaled snook, we just take one fillet off and leave the backbone attached to the other. Then simply remove the head and any guts and rinse well before marinating.

INGREDIENTS:

- 4-5 fresh snook, heads removed, halved and gutted (skin left on)
- Approximately 2 litres of water (½ litre boiling, 1½ litres cold; or you can try replacing a cup of water with a cup of Port for extra depth of flavour)
- ½ cup of firmly packed brown sugar (in other words, well pushed down)
- ½ cup of cooking salt

METHOD:

1. Place the salt and brown sugar in a large rectangular dish or container – big enough to allow the fish to be fully submerged.
2. Pour over the boiling water and stir well until sugar and salt is dissolved.
3. Add the cold water (and Port if using) and stir well. Allow to cool.
4. Submerge the fish in the brine. Cover and refrigerate for at least 4 hours or preferably overnight.
5. Next day, remove the fish and drain very, very well on a wire cake cooling rack or with paper towel.
6. Place the fish in single layers on the racks of your smoke box.
7. Smoke according to your smoker's directions and your personal taste. Our smoker usually uses 2 methylated spirit burns (we turn the fish half way through) which normally takes approximately 1½-2 hours all up.
8. Store in a brown paper bag in the fridge. Yuuuuummmm!

Marinated Tuna Steaks (GF)

It's not too often we get our hands on fresh tuna, but when we do, we make the most of it. This is a perfect Summer 'do ahead' dinner party recipe, leaving only the marinating and cooking of the steaks until last. It is a delicious marinade for green prawns as well. Serve with Mango Salsa and Mango Chutney Glaze or just enjoy as it is. Make sure you check your sauce ingredients if you have a gluten free visitor.

- 4 tuna steaks

TUNA MARINADE INGREDIENTS:

- 2 tablespoons of sesame oil
- 1 tablespoon of peanut or vegetable oil (check for allergies)
- 2 teaspoons of gluten free soy sauce
- The juice of 1 lime (or lemon)
- 1 teaspoon of gluten free fish sauce
- Some finely diced red chilli
- 1 clove of garlic, peeled and crushed
- 1 stalk of lemongrass (bottom white part only) peeled and finely chopped
- Some freshly chopped coriander
- 1 teaspoon of finely chopped ginger
- 2 teaspoons of grated palm sugar or 2 teaspoons of normal sugar

METHOD:

1. Combine all marinade ingredients and give a taste test, adding more of the sweet (sugar) sour (juice) or salt (fish sauce) to your liking.
2. Add the tuna, coating both sides and marinate for no more than 20 minutes as the marinade will start to cook the fish. Discard the remaining marinade.
3. Cook your tuna steaks on a hot grill for 3-4 minutes each side, or to your preference. Make sure if you are using a griddle style pan (with rungs) that you press down a little on the fish to create those nice grill marks.
4. Remove and leave to rest for a minute or so before serving.

Mango Salsa (GF)

INGREDIENTS:

- 1–2 mangoes, diced (or 1 x 425 gram can of mango cheeks)
- About a teaspoon of red chilli, diced
- Some fresh coriander, roughly chopped
- ½ a small red onion, peeled and diced
- 1 small Lebanese cucumber, unpeeled and diced
- 2 teaspoons of lemon or lime juice
- 2 teaspoons of grated palm sugar (or 2 teaspoons of normal sugar)

METHOD:

1. Combine all ingredients. Serve at room temperature on top of tuna steaks.

Seafood Made Simple

Mango Chutney Glaze (GF)

- 6 tablespoons of mango chutney
- Juice and zest of one small lemon
- 1 tablespoon of vegetable oil

1. Place the chutney and zest in a glass jug and purée with your hand blender.
2. Combine and heat all of the ingredients except for the oil.
3. Push the glaze through a fine sieve to remove any lumps. Stir in the oil.
4. Drizzle over the plate before adding the tuna steaks and topping with the mango salsa. You will find that it is easier to drizzle the glaze with a spoon if it is warm. Add a slice of lemon or lime on the side.

How to Butterfly Fillet Garfish

I need to precede this by saying that before leaving the ocean, we slide our hands up and down the fish in the shallows to remove their scales. We also push down below the underside of the head, right through the belly section, to push their innards out of their bottoms. This makes things much cleaner and easier when you get home to fillet.

1. Cut the head off behind the front gill then shorten your grip on your knife blade and enter above the backbone at the head end of the fish. Cut carefully down towards the tail end until you are *almost* all the way through to the belly side.

2. Turn the fish over and repeat on the other side. At this point you will only have the backbone attached by a thin strip of flesh.

3. Using your thumb, ease the backbone carefully away from the fillet.

4. To finish, remove the tiny fins at the end of the belly and clean up any black gut residue that may be left on the fillets.

Beer Battered Garfish

Of course you can use beer batter with any kind of fish, I just particularly like it with garfish which is best deep-fried to dissolve all their bones. The other reason is that it gives us a good excuse to go dabbing for garfish on warm Summer nights– one of my all-time favourite activities.

INGREDIENTS:

- An equal quantity of Cornflour and Plain flour
  (the Cornflour will give a lovely light texture to the batter)
- Part of a can of beer (don't worry - there will be some left for you)
- 1 teaspoon of vinegar
- Freshly ground salt and pepper
- 1 egg, separated
- Local fishing expert 'Plover' recommends adding a pinch or two of curry powder for extra colour and flavour, optional
- Filleted garfish, or fish of your choice
- Vegetable oil for deep-frying

METHOD:

1. Place your deep-frying oil on to heat. You will know when it is hot enough as food will sizzle on contact. Don't allow it to get smoking hot.
2. Combine dry ingredients in a shallow plate or dish.
3. Gradually add splashes of beer and the beaten egg yolk and whisk with a fork until you reach the right consistency – like thin sunscreen. Do not apply - we have spoken about this before! Whisk the egg white separately until light and fluffy and then fold gently into the batter mixture. The batter should be just thick enough not to drip off the fish. Stir in the vinegar.
4. Coat fish on both sides and then deep-fry them in the hot vegetable oil until golden. This will take between 2 and 4 minutes, depending on their size. I prefer to use my deep-fryer without the basket for frying fish as the batter tends to get stuck between the wire. Of course you could also cook them in a frying pan.
5. Drain, season with salt and serve immediately.

Seafood Made Simple

Tender Squid Every Time

Now I don't want to sound like a mass murderer, but as with most living produce, the tenderness of the flesh is largely dependent on the speed and manner in which it met its demise. Graphic as this may sound, it's true. The humble squid is no different.

When you reel in your squid, use your hand to firmly squeeze the part where the neck joins the body, and hold tightly until the flesh turns white – about 4-5 seconds. This method essentially strangles the squid and results in lovely tender calamari every time, whether it's fresh from the sea or straight out of the freezer. No need for milk or the mallet.

Bear in mind that when you are reeling it in, there is a high probability that you will end up wearing the ink, hence it is advisable to wear old clothes!

How to Clean Calamari (Squid)

This is my favourite seafood cleaning task – there's just something about the slippery, sensory experience that I love.

Seafood Made Simple

How to Clean Calamari (Squid)...

1. Use your fingers to push down behind the head inside the tube and gently separate the cartilage (clear back bone) from the body of the squid.

2. Simultaneously pull the head and the end of the body to remove the head and innards of the squid from its body. If you are lucky, this will come out cleanly without too much inky mess.

3. Remove the flaps (or wings) from the body by easing your fingers and thumb in between the two. Then take off the outer skins of each, discarding any slimy bits.

4. Turn the hood inside out to ensure it is thoroughly clean. You do this by pressing your thumb into the tip of the body and pushing it inside itself with the use of your other hand. Cut to your desired shape.

5. Whether or not you eat the tentacles is up to you. We do, but we always remove the tips of the two long ones as they can be pretty tough - the heads we freeze for the burley pot – waste not, want not.

Seafood Made Simple

Salt and Pepper Squid

INGREDIENTS:

- Cleaned and well drained calamari, cut into the desired shape and size (too much moisture on the calamari will cause spitting during the frying process)
- Combination of half Plain flour and half Cornflour (start with ½ a cup of each)
- A good teaspoon of ground black peppercorns
- A few good grindings of salt
- Canola or vegetable oil for deep-frying

METHOD:

1. Place your deep-fryer and vegetable oil on to heat. Food should sizzle on contact when the oil is hot enough but do not allow it to get smoking hot.
2. Place all of the dry ingredients into a plastic container or bag.
3. Add the calamari, small amounts at a time, and toss well. Repeat until all calamari is coated.
4. Gently lower small amounts of the calamari into the hot oil (it's up to you if you use the basket or not). Fry for 1-2 minutes or until just golden. Repeat with remaining calamari and serve immediately. Alternatively you could shallow-fry them in a pan.

How to Shuck an Oyster

First and foremost, invest in an oyster shucker and possibly a set of strong leather gloves if you are the DA type.

1. Hold the oyster firmly in your left hand (for right handers) dome side against your palm.

2. Carefully insert the blade of your shucker at about 3 o'clock. Gently lever it back and forth until the lid of the shell gives way. This can be where a glove can come in handy to avoid you requiring urgent medical attention! Remove the lid and discard.

3. Use the blade of your shucker to delicately cut the muscle on the underside of the oyster, from where it attaches to the shell. This ensures that it will easily slip out of the shell regardless of whether you are eating them natural or cooked.

Oysters Kilpatrick

Oysters Kilpatrick always sparks a bit of controversy as everyone seems to have a different opinion on what should go in the mix. Therefore, rather than give you a fixed recipe, I will provide you with some options and let you experiment or make your own choices! Without a doubt no one ever disputes the fact that there is bacon in the dish – as for the rest?

POSSIBLE INGREDIENTS:

Freshly shucked oysters in their shell, diced bacon, grated cheese, Worcestershire sauce, tomato sauce, BBQ sauce, a pinch of brown sugar, Tabasco sauce (if you like a 'kick'), very finely diced red onion, bread crumbs, fresh parsley, cream, coarse rock salt for sprinkling and as a bed for serving (optional) and fresh lemon wedges for serving.

Personally, my mixture would include diced bacon and onion, grated cheese, a drop or two of Tabasco sauce, a pinch of brown sugar, tomato sauce, a good shake of Worcestershire sauce and sometimes a dash of cream.

METHOD:

1. Preheat the griller or BBQ hotplate.
2. Place opened oysters, in their shell, on a heat-proof tray. I usually use a tray with small sides as this gives the oysters something to lean against. It is also quite safe to nestle them in rock salt and place that under the griller.
3. Prepare your own concoction of toppings in a small bowl. If using bread crumbs, these would be sprinkled on top just before grilling with the cheese over the top.
4. Place a teaspoon of your mixture into each shell and then cook under the griller until golden and the oyster is cooked through. Don't overcook.

Seafood Made Simple

So You've Got Crabs?!#

Though not something you might admit in a crowd, these under-sea creatures are a culinary delight.

My brother Dene lives in Far North Queensland and enjoys nothing more than crabbing in the crocodile infested rivers and creeks near his home at beautiful Mission Beach. Neil and I looked on with some fascination as Dene proceeded to share with us (and now I with you) his crab tying technique. It was not crab season when we visited, so the crab pictured here was a 'catch and release' morsel for modelling purposes only.

Tying the crabs helps to stop them from fighting and losing limbs. It also makes them much easier to handle of course and they can also be cooked whilst they are tied. The same technique is used for tying other varieties of crabs.

We initially thought my brother having bare feet in the boat was just his own personal take on his hippie/semi-retired lifestyle (check out the headband!) so we therefore opted to keep our shoes on. However we had to eat our words when he went on to show how skilful the human big toe can be; no matter how hairy, black or disfigured it is.

Crabs can stay alive for up to a week if stored in an esky under a wet, cool bag but generally speaking they will need to be tied up so they don't attack each other.

As with any form of recreational fishing, be sure to always check the legal size and bag limits for your area and the variety of crabs you are catching, cause if you think the crab pots and beer were expensive for the day, that will be nothing compared to the cost of the fine!

Also, leave the girls (Jennies) alone so they can breed up for next year. The females usually have a wider dome-shaped flap on the underside of their shell whilst the boys are more triangular. If you catch a crab that has bright orange or yellow eggs under their back, throw them back. Crabs displaying a pale mustard colour underneath should also be released as this can be caused by a parasite.

Here Dene walks us through his delicate labour of love.

For those who are yet to enjoy the monster Mud Crabs that inhabit our Northern Australian estuaries, buy yourself a crab pot in Far North Queensland and head to almost any crocodile infested waterway as they are also home to our famous Mud Crabs. Of course all due care must be exercised to ensure that any baiting is for the crabs, and that you do not become the bait for the larger inhabitants of the waterways.

Tying Crabs

1. Cut a piece of string approximately 2 – 3 foot long (about a metre). Place your bare foot firmly on top of the back of the crab. It is not possible to have control over the crab if you have shoes on. He will be much more likely to get away and bite you. Folklore says that the big nipper can crack the top off a long neck.

2. Drape the string around the front of the shell and under the mouth, pulling it in a sawing type motion to make sure it comes right into the underside of the shell as shown in the photo. At this stage you should have an even amount of string in each hand while you are controlling the crab with your foot. Held like this, he cannot bite you.

3. As shown in the photo, you must now bring each side of your string around the back and under the base of the shell and then forward and up under the pincers. Locate the notch at the rear of the upper pincers to keep your string in place. This is best accomplished doing one side at a time and it is important to pull the nippers in tight against the crab's body while keeping the string tight at the same time. You are now entering the danger zone where things are most likely to go pear shaped, so don't be fooled into thinking that the crabs will just sit there and take it!

4. Figure four shows the correct position of the string. From this point onwards it is critical to keep the tension on the string, pulling it back towards your foot.

5. Bring each side of your string back over the top of the shell and thread between the back and 2nd leg. Pull the string into the middle and continue to keep it tight.

6. Now this is the tricky part (if you didn't think it was tricky enough already). You must turn the crab on its back whilst at the same time keeping the string tight and tie a knot to keep it restrained. This takes practice, however the secret is in your toes! When you are tying the knot, use your toe to keep the first tie tight and in place. Then tie your final knot which should slip under your toe as you tighten it. It is now time to repeat the process with your remaining crabs whilst you contemplate how good they will taste with a few cold beers.

Seafood Made Simple

Cleaning up Your Crabs – No Antibiotics Involved!

OK, so you've caught your crabs; here's what to do next.
For this demonstration I am using Blue Swimmer Crabs.

As with mud crabs, the males are determined by a triangular shaped flap on the underside rather than a rounded domed flap on the girls. The adult males also have much brighter shells and claws than the females. Again, make sure you check the laws in your area relating to limits.

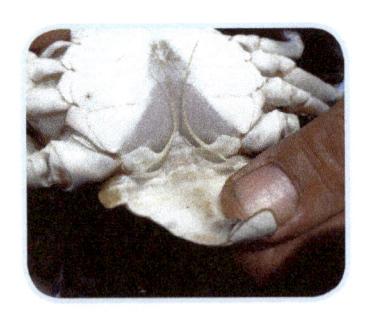

1. Fold down the triangular flap on the underside of the body.

2. Pull this flap back to separate the shell from the body by opening it up like a compact. Try to scoop out most of the innards with the shell as you remove it. If you like you can save the top of the shell for presentation. Alternatively most of the discarded pieces of crab shell can be used to make a great stock.

3. Remove the eyes and antennae from the head.

4. Remove the side bits of flesh (inedible gills) and the innards from the centre of the crab. Give a light rinse and cook whole or cut into smaller pieces if desired. It pays to crack the big legs and nippers of the crabs before cooking to allow the flavours to seep in and out and also for ease of eating.

52　Seafood Made Simple

Cooking Crabs

Some people put their crabs on ice or in the freezer for a while prior to cooking. They do this to slow down their metabolism, the theory being it is less of a shock to them when cooking and therefore more humane. Well 'hello' but sorry fellas – there ain't no avoiding the next step either way. The most humane way to kill them is to freeze them alive which means that when you thaw them, you can clean them properly before you cook them rather than the other way around. How you choose to go about it doesn't change the end result.

METHOD:

1. Bring some salty water to the boil in a large saucepan. You don't need to completely cover the crabs, as the steam will do the job and it will make the cooking process quicker.
2. Leave the lid three quarters of the way on the pot and boil for approximately twenty minutes or until the crabs have turned red and the flesh inside is white. Average sized Mud Crabs take around 20 minutes but cooking time will vary depending on the size and variety of the crabs.
3. Dunk the cooked crabs into some icy cold water immediately after cooking as this helps to 'set' the meat and keep the crabs nice and juicy.

Beer Steamed Blueys (Blue Swimmer Crabs)

We don't often catch crabs (no jokes please) but this is an excellent Summer BBQ recipe to impress your friends. You will need some sort of high domed lid or large metal bowl/saucepan to be able to turn upside down under which to steam the crabs on the hotplate. You can cook these equally well in a wok. Adjust the chilli levels to your liking.

INGREDIENTS:

- 4-6 blue swimmer crabs, cleaned, claws cracked and bodies cut into halves (you could substitute mud crabs if you like and you may choose to leave a couple whole for looks)
- 1 cup of tomato sauce
- 1 onion, peeled and finely diced
- 1 clove of garlic, peeled and crushed
- ½ large red capsicum, deseeded and very finely sliced
- A small dessertspoon of freshly grated ginger (or you could use a teaspoon of ginger powder)
- The zest and juice of half a lemon
- 1 tablespoon of Sambal Olek paste (Indonesian spicy chilli paste)
- 1 long red spur chilli, deseeded and finely sliced
- A good splash of sesame or vegetable oil
- Salt and black pepper
- 1 can of your favourite beer – half for you, the rest for the crabs
- A bunch of spring onions or coriander, chopped – to use as a garnish

Note: To crack the crab claws you can either use some clean pliers or the edge of a meat mallet.

METHOD:

1. Combine all ingredients (except for the beer and spring onions) into a large bowl or pot and then add the crabs and toss well. Refrigerate for at least an hour to allow the flavours to go through.
2. Crank up your solid BBQ plate (or wok) to a medium heat and carefully pour on your crab mixture. Place your heat-proof lid or bowl on top and gradually add small amounts of beer under the lid, remembering to save a sip or two for yourself. Lift the lid and stir every few minutes so the crabs cook evenly.
3. When the crabs are cooked through and have turned white in the thickest part of the flesh, serve scattered with chopped spring onions (or coriander) and some extra wedges of lemon.

How to Peel a Prawn

For all you ladies (or snaggy type guys) who don't want to get your hands dirty – get over yourself. Part of the pleasure of our wonderful seafood is the anticipation of putting it in your mouth.

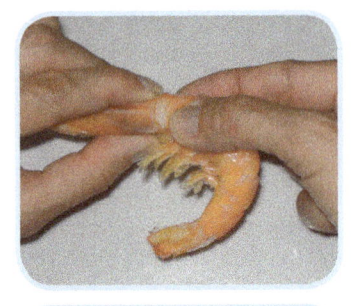

1. Hold the head of the prawn with one hand and use your other hand to twist the body clockwise to detach it from the head. Discard the head or keep it for making stock.

2. Use your fingers to rip off the little 'feet' on the underside of the body.

3. Carefully peel the layer of shell off.

4. Gently pull the line of 'pooh' out, starting from the head end. Rinse only if necessary.

Note: For the peeling and eating process, a lot of people have a little finger bowl ready for hand rinsing between prawns. Otherwise don't underestimate the usefulness of a cheap tissue or serviette.

Specky Prawn and Nectarine Salad (GF)

If you don't have fresh nectarines, mangoes are a great substitute.

INGREDIENTS:

- Desired amount of cooked and peeled prawns
- Desired amount of freshly sliced nectarines (or mangoes)
- ½ red capsicum, thinly sliced
- Some fresh avocado slices, optional
- Some fresh greens eg lettuce, baby spinach, beetroot leaves etc
- Dressing (see below)

DRESSING INGREDIENTS:

- 1 teaspoon of grated, fresh ginger (or ½ teaspoon of powdered ginger)
- ½ cup of oil
- 2 tablespoons of white vinegar
- 1½ tablespoons of honey
- 1 teaspoon of seeded mustard (½ teaspoon of dry mustard for the gluten free)
- 3 teaspoons of lemon juice
- 1 tablespoon of finely chopped fresh chives
- 1 teaspoon of finely chopped fresh dill

METHOD:

1. Combine all dressing ingredients in a jar or container with a lid and shake well.
2. Prepare prawns.
3. Slice nectarines, capsicum and avocado (if using) and pour the desired amount of dressing over the top immediately to avoid discolouration.
4. Add the prawns and serve immediately.

Note: *This is a great dinner party recipe as it is both fresh and fast to prepare. The dressing will keep for some time in a jar in the fridge and the prawns and fruits are very quick to assemble.*

Prawn Laksa

This is a basic Laksa soup which is usually made with either seafood or chicken.

INGREDIENTS:

- 5-6 tablespoons of Laksa paste (a red paste which comes in a jar, found in the Oriental section at the shop)
- 2 teaspoons of oil for frying
- 2 x (400 ml) tins of coconut milk
- 1 large can of bean sprouts, drained (or fresh if you have them)
- Some seafood of your choice such as prawns - you can use 'green' (raw) or cooked
- 2 wads of vermicelli rice noodles
- Some boiling water
- Fresh coriander for serving, optional

METHOD:

1. Place the oil in a saucepan and add the Laksa paste.
2. Stir for a minute or two until the paste is simmering (small bubbles) and becomes very fragrant (in other words stronger in smell – not unlike you)!
3. Pour in the coconut milk and bring to the boil.
4. Add the seafood and bring to the boil and serve. If using 'green' seafood you will need to let the soup come to the boil and simmer until the meat turns white – usually 2-4 minutes.
5. Place the vermicelli noodles in a bowl and cover with boiling water. Leave to sit for 2-3 minutes and then tip into a colander and rinse under cold water to stop the cooking process. Allow to drain.
6. Divide noodles and bean sprouts evenly between serving bowls.
7. Pour Laksa over the noodles and sprouts and garnish with coriander. Serves 4.

How to Cook and Clean Yabbies

We often enjoy a feed of our local yabbies while camping. They are very similar to the Red Claw that are caught in the more tropical areas of Australia and are both pretty much cooked and peeled in exactly the same way as prawns.

One yabbier's guide to preparing them for cooking is as follows: Animal rights people stop reading now. They swear that the meat has a clean fresh flavour free from mud, which can often be the case when cooking them whole.

METHOD:

1. Take the live yabbie and twist its head from the body. A bit gross I know.
2. Grab the centre tail flap and pull it away from the body, easing out the 'pooh track' as you go.
3. Place them into boiling salted water (along with any large claws) and bring the water back to the boil. Cook for 3–5 minutes, depending on their size, before removing and refreshing in ice cold water. The meat turns white when cooked. Alternatively you can throw them straight on the BBQ like this.

Sam's Pickled Yabbies (GF)

My nephew is an expert yabbier and often brings a jar of the pickled morsels to family gatherings.

INGREDIENTS:

- A quantity of cooked and cleaned yabbies
- Equal quantities of white and spiced vinegar
- Some finely chopped red chilli
- Black peppercorns
- Some peeled and sliced garlic cloves
- 1 dessertspoon of sugar (per jar)
- Some fresh coriander, optional

METHOD:

1. Heat the vinegar and sugar in a saucepan or the microwave then stir until the sugar has dissolved. Allow to cool before adding the other ingredients.
2. Place the prepared yabbies into a clean jam jar (or jars) with a metal screw top lid.
3. Use the above mixture to completely cover the cooked yabbies and seal well. Refrigerate.

Note: If you want to keep them for any length of time, the jar and lid will need to be well sterilised (see instructions in the preserving section).

Zombie's Tips for Cooking Crayfish

Our South Australian ocean is certainly home to some of the world's finest seafood and crayfish is no exception. As we rarely get to see one of these tasty morsels I headed to a friend for some advice.

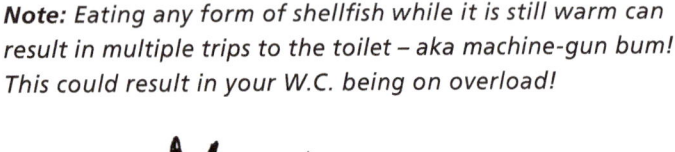

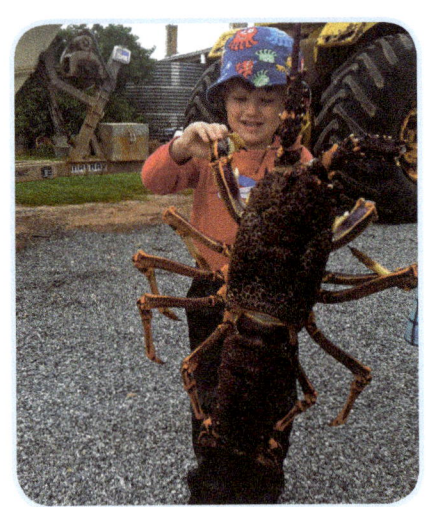

1. Weigh your catch. This will tell you how long you will need to cook them.
2. Heat enough sea water (or salted water) in a large saucepan to more than cover your crayfish. Bring it to the boil.
3. Meanwhile prepare an ice cold water bath. Not for you – to refresh the crayfish.
4. Place crayfish in the pot and bring back to the boil. Continue to boil for 1 minute per 100 grams. You will notice that it turns a brilliant orangey red colour.
5. Carefully remove from the water with tongs and dunk immediately into ice water for 2-3 minutes. This helps to set the meat and stop it from overcooking. Some people like to add ice to seawater to retain that ocean flavour or alternatively you can cool them down in the ocean itself.
6. Allow to cool and then refrigerate before eating.
7. Best enjoyed on a remote beach with your fishing mates and a nice cold beer.

Note: Eating any form of shellfish while it is still warm can result in multiple trips to the toilet – aka machine-gun bum! This could result in your W.C. being on overload!

58   Seafood Made Simple

Camping Capers

What type of camper are you? P.S. It doesn't pay to get too comfortable on your deck chair

What type of Camper are you?

As I sit here at the keyboard, I am contemplating our much awaited annual Easter camping trip, so what better headset to be in when talking about the importance of a little bit of organisation and some smart packing.

I seriously can't help but chuckle as I think about the differences in all of us, which become particularly apparent during the 'argumentative set up phase'. The really sneaky ones like to get there first so that no one else gets to see them set up. Then they can enjoy relaxing in their deck chairs with a nice cold beverage and watch as the floor show unfolds around them. OK, firstly you need to understand which category of camper you fall into; only then will you know if it is worth reading on.

THE ANALIST!

(These campers border on being 'anal' but get an 'A' for their organisation. They can commonly be a pain in the a*se for other campers and, if you haven't guessed by now, we fall into this category).

Analists are communicators and usually establish if their group are going to do their own food thing on the trip or if they are in fact going to work together. This way they plan to take enough, but not too much. They carry all of the necessary equipment and put a great deal of thought into their packing. Initial setting up is a methodical activity, which if done correctly, makes the rest of the trip a breeze.

They are highly likely to be able to produce any given piece of equipment on request but sometimes fall to pieces when things don't go to plan. On the upside, they are often relied upon by other campers when they run into trouble.

BEHIND THE 8 BALLERS!

(Not always a lot of communication, thought or preparation is involved when it comes to organisation)!

Behind the 8 Ballers are those misguided, non-communicative campers who seriously believe that they will eat their way through 18 packets of BBQ meat, 8 dips, 26 packets of biscuits, 6 blocks of cheese and four cartons of beer in 2 nights. OK well the beer maybe. That makes them the same campers who end up going home with an esky full of soggy meat and food that needs to be dealt with (or worse still, thrown out) because every other camper on the trip brought a ridiculous amount of perishable food as well.

They usually pack 10 minutes after knocking off work and 30 minutes before leaving on the trip, making a stop at the shop and the bottle O on the way. These campers often have no idea how to erect their tent or use their equipment, as that was another thing they bought on the way. They will often have to rely on the assistance of *The Analists* to get them out of trouble.

A prime example of the *Behind the 8 Ballers* trap can be demonstrated in a phone call from one young lady who was also going camping for Easter.

She said to me "I don't know how I am going to fit everything in. I need this, and this and this and this…" And on and on she went…Did I say she went on and on?

I replied "How many other people are going?"

"Thirteen."

"Well do you think any of them might have some of those things?"

"Well how would I know, they don't talk!"

Communication! I rest my case.

THE NATURALIST!

(Not to be confused with 'naturist' as they are naked. Naturalists are haters of needless clutter and time wasting organisational tasks).

The Naturalist relies heavily on nature (and in some cases God) to provide for them. They are devoid of all accessories and rely (sometimes to a delusional extent) on their own skill and knowledge. This can let them down sadly when the fish are not biting.

Whilst great in theory, they may end up enjoying nothing more than cold shoulder for tea and are in some danger of starvation or dehydration.

Naturalists watch on in fascination from their drift rope hammocks, while *The Analists, Behind the 8 Ballers* and *The Precious Ones* go through the 'argumentative set up phase'. Whilst most of their problems transpire later in the trip when it comes to what to eat and where to sleep. However, they are not totally immune from arguments themselves, unless of course they are travelling solo.

THE PRECIOUS ONES!

(Are commonly spotted in fresh clothes everyday often white – and dirt and germs are their arch enemies).

Precious Ones can often border on obsessive compulsive with their behaviour and the constant need to clean and sanitise their whole camping experience. Fastidious about everything from their nails and clothing to who's using their equipment, they are a great source of amusement to all other campers. Bathing and toileting are right up there as high priorities for *The Precious Ones* and there has been many a throne erected to appease their royal butts. Some may say it may have been easier (and more hygienic) to stay home.

THE FIVE STAR CAMPERS!

(We have no such experiences with campers of this calibre as they are way out of our budget and league – 5 star vans and Winnebagos hardly fall into the camping category).

After reading this there is no doubt that you will have had a good laugh and spent some time on self-analysis (where you probably noticed you overlapped into different categories yourself); at least you can laugh about the fact that there are always a few good stories to come out of every camping adventure.

Food Tips When Camping

Aaahh (sigh) camping. There is just something about being out in the great outdoors that takes my interest in food to a whole new level. Firstly, you've often got a lot more time on your hands which makes food preparation much less stressful and downright enjoyable; and secondly, you are often driven to cook by hunger and lack of convenience stores.

Camping is also an important time to consider your food choices, pack smart and experiment with what you've got, or can catch. Though don't be fooled into thinking that any hunting attempts will necessarily be successful, as many a fisherman has come home and had to contemplate eating his bait.

This brings me to the subject of what to pack. Now I admit that I am somewhat 'anal' with my packing when it comes to food and that I am well aware that you can just as easily survive on tinned meat and baked beans.

Now, when I talk about preparing food for camping, I am assuming that there is no shop nearby and that the trip is limited to a weekend or several days at most. Naturally long term camping requires much more thought and preparation.

My food tips for camping start with packing as many dry and non-perishable items as you can and making the absolute most of your cold space which is usually your biggest issue.

In the Esky or Fridge:

- Pack long life milk, preferably in smaller sized containers if you are not big milk drinkers, as small 'juice size' milk will take up less room in a car fridge or esky when opened. Obviously you do not need to put this in the fridge until after you have opened it. Then, simply open another one when it runs out. The same applies to things like orange juice; buy two small instead of one large.
- Only put a few drinks on ice to start with and then keep topping up your supply as you drink them. I've seen a lot of eskies with heaps of booze in them and little room for the more sustaining items such as food. Get your priorities right. It's smarter to have a whole other esky dedicated to the all-important beverages.
- Instead of taking big bottles of things like salad dressings, sauce and the likes, transfer them to smaller containers. Square stackable ones with lids are great because they take up a lot less room. Don't underestimate the food, space and longer-term money saving benefits of using containers.
- I like to put any fresh fruit and vegetables into a large plastic container with a good sealing lid for three reasons.

One; when you go to find your veggies in the esky they are all in the one spot. This makes sense as you often need numerous vegetables at any one time when cooking.
Two; they will stay a lot fresher for longer.
Three; it's not that practical to have small items like cucumbers etc rolling around in between other items, or worse still, floating in melted ice.

62   Camping Capers

You will find you make the most of your cold space this way and there will be a lot less digging around. For these reasons it is worth the small investment to buy a few decent sized containers that will fit in your esky or fridge. If you can't afford containers, then you've clearly got more problems than what you can and can't fit in your cooler for a start. Then use some good sealing plastic bags to keep things fresh and together. I sometimes pre-cut some salad items and store them in a plastic bag so I can just grab the 'salad bag' and add the last minute ingredients and dressing.

General Food Packing Tips:

- First and foremost, make sure you have plenty of fresh drinking water. Man cannot live on beer alone. Mmm, debatable!

- Freezing clean milk or juice containers for ice can give you additional drinking water when they have thawed. Or, freeze the milk or juice itself and kill two birds with one stone.

- Take a good supply of hard vegetables which do not need refrigeration. These include potatoes, onions, carrots, whole pumpkins, turnips etc. These veggies are perfect for stews and soups etc and can survive without refrigeration for a few days if kept in a cool place.

- Pack dried or canned foods wherever possible. Canned veggies are a great alternative to fresh and if you don't use them, nothing lost. Better still are dried ones, which you can reconstitute by adding water, which makes them swell back to their original size. They are much lighter and take up less room.

- It's worth dedicating a little space for a few condiments like stock cubes and some basic herbs and sauces. Those I wouldn't leave home without are Worcestershire, tomato, chilli and soy sauce, and herbs such as rosemary, basil, garlic, lemon pepper, thyme, parsley and whatever else takes your fancy. Of course fresh is best but I must assume that many of you are either not gardeners, or can't be bothered forking out the money for fresh herbs. I keep my fresh herbs in a plastic container in my fridge when I have them. These little babies will be worth their weight in gold when it comes to turning all that leftover meat into a great stew in the camp oven. And of course, don't forget the salt and pepper.

- Take some extra plastic containers with lids for putting things like opened biscuits into, to keep them nice and fresh. Dewy biscuits at 7 am are about as appealing as looking in the mirror after a night on the booze. Lots of the cheap shops have suitable bowls with lids which stack inside each other and save heaps of space. They also double as salad and mixing bowls if needed.

- And finally, unless you want to come home the size of an elephant, take a few last moments to reconsider just how much perishable food and grog you really need passing your lips (and then ending up on your hips) and then take off 20%. This is how much to pack. The one exception to this rule is if you are planning on catching some of your food. In this instance it is highly advisable to pack a little extra, just in case luck is not on your side. Generally speaking I have never met a camper yet who ran out of food.

The Humble Ironing Board

The multi-functional uses of the humble ironing board on the camping trip simply cannot be overstated. If you have the space to pack one (and remember that they fold down flat for easy transportation) you will be rewarded with one of the cheapest and most versatile pieces of camping equipment ever. Best of all, you could probably pick one up at a garage sale for next to nothing.

THE PORTABLE BAR
Don't waste a drop.

FISH CLEANING TABLE
In or out of the water.

THE CAMPFIRE COMPANION
Perfect for the hot stuff.

THE CLOTHES AIRER

SELF-DRAINING DISH RACK
Though they may drain themselves unfortunately the same can't be said for the washing.

THE BARBIE MATE
Next to the BBQ stand using unique dumb a*se ingenuity.

THE MULTI-HEIGHT COFFEE TABLE Perfect for entertaining.

Note: For uses requiring extra stability, simply drill some holes in the legs and secure into the ground with some extra tent pegs. Definitely a camping must.

64 Camping Capers

Getting Gassed and Connected

(Not to be confused with getting drunk and trying to pick up!)

Before we can embark on cooking, we need to establish that you do in fact know how to light a barbeque. Now most blokes might scoff at this, but there are plenty of guys and girls out there who could do with a little help in this department, after all; playing with gas and matches can present some problems for the novice – including giving them an instant hair and brow trim. If all else fails, ring Dad for help.

Beware too that there are some areas and conditions that may prohibit you from operating even a gas BBQ so make sure you check first.

Getting Gassed!

Most gas outlets have a swap-and-go system in Australia which means you take your empty bottle in, pay, and they replace it with a full bottle on the spot. Gas bottles all have an expiry date on the bottom after which time they will not be refilled. They also need to be in good condition before retailers will swap them.

You can determine how much gas you have in your bottle in several ways, but at the end of the day, when the gas runs out, so does your cooking.

- Gas is heavier than air, so if you know how much your gas bottle weighs and it's feeling pretty light, chances are you are running low.
- Sometimes if you give it a shake you can feel the gas moving in the bottle.
- Gas is cooler than air, so if the lower half of the bottle is cold and the other half is room temperature, your bottle is probably only half full.

Camping Capers

Getting Connected

Now that you have established that you have gas in your bottle, it's time to get connected. Making sure that the gas gets from the bottle to the BBQ needs some careful attention. Knowing which bit goes where is important.

There is an old saying about taps; 'Lefty Lighty, Righty Tighty'. In other words, turning to the left releases or opens something, while turning to the right, tightens or closes it. This applies to gas bottles too but there are always arrows on the top of your cylinder to help you if you get confused. Obviously you have the gas turned to off (or closed) while you are getting connected.

1. Ensure your gas bottle is in the 'closed' or 'off' position. Some bottles have a regulator attached. A regulator delivers a controlled amount of gas to the burner allowing for consistent heat during the cooking process.

2. Make sure that your hoses are properly attached between the gas bottle and the BBQ. When in place and ready to cook, turn the gas bottle to the 'open' or 'on' position before proceeding to light.

Note: Whenever your BBQ is not in use, your gas bottle should be turned off.

Lighting Up

SELF IGNITING BBQS:

- This style of BBQ has an automatic pilot for the gas and does not need matches or a gas gun to light. Once you have the gas connected and turned on, you simply push the burner knob in and hold while turning until you hear the ignition switch click and the flame start. Some BBQ's have a separate ignition button to push in at the same time as turning the knob. Sometimes this may take several goes. Once alight, you can let the knob go.

GAS BURNERS AND BBQS WITHOUT AUTOMATIC IGNITION:

- These BBQ's and burners require you to turn the gas bottle on and then strike a match (or safer still, use a gas gun) to ignite the flame. Much care needs to be taken not to give yourself third degree burns and make sure the gas is only on for a few seconds at a time if your first ignition fails.
- Too much gas in the air + naked flame = flame grilled 'Dumb A*se'!

66   Camping Capers

A Word on Fire Lighting

Do not proceed to light any fires without making sure you are aware of any regulations for your particular area, daily weather forecast and time of year, as the consequences can be not only catastrophic, but very expensive. Even gas barbecues are subject to restrictions and regulations in some instances.

Then, unless you are willing to spend copious amounts of time rubbing two sticks together (gaining blisters and RSI at best) don't forget to pack the matches.

We will then assume that you have access to dry wood and kindling. And whilst on the subject of wood, pleeeease don't go ripping down every dry stick you find without checking first on what firewood regulations there are, if any, in your area. Don't underestimate the assistance that may also be obtained from man's best friend when it comes to collecting firewood.

Fires primarily need three things – fuel (in the way of wood and kindling), air and a degree of skill and technique (of which my husband tells me I have very little - and I tell him that if I was any good at it – I wouldn't need him).

Tips on Fire Lighting

Building a fire is somewhat like building a pyramid – start from the bottom and work up.

Most fires, especially ones on which you intend to cook, benefit from being sunk into a shallow hole. This helps to reduce the effects of wind, while also keeping your coals together and out of the way of stray feet around the campfire.

- Begin with some scrunched up dry paper or a wad of dead grass.
- On top of this, place some dead leaves and fine, dry sticks.
- Begin building your pyramid of larger sticks and logs over and around your base, leaving space for the air to get through them. You don't want to put a big log or stump directly on top of your fire as this will only cause it to smoke, thus extinguishing any chance of a flame. This is a common rookie mistake.
- Once your fire is established, you can add the big stuff. And there you go – Bob's your uncle.

If all else fails, pack the firelighters, or in the case of farmers – petrol (caution required).

Fire Safety

It is imperative (meaning very, very important) that you make sure all campfires are extinguished and/or covered when finished with. Uncovered campfires can turn catastrophic the next morning, particularly at the beach, when the still-hot coals look the same as the sand.

Camping Capers

Camp Oven Apricot Chicken with Rosemary (GF)

You can cook this on top of a bed of coals, or you can place the camp oven directly on top of the hot plate.

INGREDIENTS:

- 3 tablespoons of oil
- 4-6 chicken Marylands (thigh and a*se section of the chicken)
- 2 large brown onions, peeled and sliced
- 2 cloves of garlic, peeled and diced
- 1 large can of apricot nectar
- 2 gluten free beef stock cubes, crumbled
- A few sprigs of rosemary
- A few sprigs of thyme
- Salt and pepper
- Some Plain flour for dusting, optional (leave this step out for the gluten free guest or replace with gluten free Plain flour)

METHOD:

1. Place flour and chicken portions in a plastic bag or container and shake well.
2. Heat oil in the camp oven and add the chicken and the sliced onion. Cook until the chicken is golden on both sides and the onions are caramelised. Add more oil if necessary.
3. Add the garlic and cook a further minute or two.
4. Add all other ingredients and place the lid on the camp oven. Cook over slow coals for approximately 30-40 minutes or until chicken is cooked through. If you have coated the chicken with Plain flour first, the sauce should thicken nicely. If not, see below.

Note: If you want to thicken the sauce (if it has not reduced enough already), mix ¼ cup water with a tablespoon of Corn or Plain flour and stir into the boiling mixture. Alternatively you could add a handful of dry rice about 10 minutes before you are ready to eat.

Jaffles

Where do I begin with Jaffles? Some people have never heard the name and would just call them toasted sandwiches; but either way they are deliciously easy, cheap and fun! Jaffle irons are readily available from camping and outdoor shops. We usually have a Jaffle night at least once a year as it beats cleaning the hot plate. They also make great square eggs for brekkie.

My only tips for cooking would be to make sure your bread is very well buttered on the sides which touch the iron (outside of sandwich) and don't have your coals too hot or they may be black on the outside and still cold in the centre. Overfilling can also be a bit of a trap.

We have an old fashioned metal wheelbarrow which makes a great fire pit for Jaffles. One, because you can rest your iron on the sides; two, because it's at the perfect level and you don't need to move from your chair; and three, it's somewhat portable – with care.

I am merely going to list some filling suggestions here, as the possibilities are infinite.

- Leftover or canned curry and rice
- Diced bacon or ham, corn and mashed potato (my niece's favourite)
- Spaghetti
- Baked beans
- Cheese
- Leftover or canned casseroles and stews
- Salamis, cold meats etc
- Leftover mornay
- Leftover potato bakes

The Bung It On Barbie!

This is one of my favourite ways to BBQ and is a great way to use up leftover stuff in your fridge or esky, especially at the end of your camping trip. The idea of this recipe is to create your own mini stir-fry creations.

Either provide or have your guests bring any of the items overleaf and have some small bowls on hand so that people can mix their own individual meals. Send them to the BBQ to 'Bung It On', stir and then eat.

People can then re-use their bowl to try out a different combo next time. Make sure you don't put your cooked food in the raw food bowl though, or only bad things will happen.

Camping Capers 71

Core Ingredient Suggestions (far from exhaustive):

MEAT SUGGESTIONS:

- Stir-fry style meats – chicken, pork, veal, lamb etc
- Seafood of your choice – prawns, calamari, mussels etc

VEGETABLE SUGGESTIONS:

- Finely shredded vegetables such as cabbage, bok choy or other leafy greens
- Bean shoots
- Canned water chestnuts (yum)
- Julienned (thin match stick style) veggies such as carrots, celery, zucchini, capsicum, squash etc
- Finely sliced or diced onion
- Snow peas, beans, baby corn etc

ADDED EXTRAS:

- A selection of nuts (as long as no one has allergies) such as cashews or peanuts – these give a delicious flavour and texture to your stir-fry
- Some cooked rice
- Some cooked noodles
- Sauces, spices and accompaniment suggestions: soy, fish, oyster, sweet chilli, black bean, BBQ, honey, lemon juice, peanut butter, ginger, garlic, coriander, lemongrass etc

Beer Bread

This is a delicious addition to any soup or stew and in my camping experience the beer is never far away.

INGREDIENTS:

- 3 cups of Self Raising flour (if you don't have Self Raising flour you can add 3 teaspoons of baking powder to Plain flour for the same result)
- 1 x 375 ml can of beer of your choice (and extra for drinking while you are waiting for the bread to cook)
- Half a handful of sugar
- A little melted butter

METHOD:

1. Combine the dry ingredients and add the beer, stirring until combined.
2. Oil a log or cake tin (or similar vessel) that will fit inside your camp oven and add your mixture. Put your tin on top of your trivet to keep it off the hot base.
3. Pour the melted butter over the top with a sprinkle of salt and place the lid on the camp oven.
4. Place the oven onto a medium bed of coals and place the lid on top. Place a few more coals on top of the lid to ensure an even heat.
5. The length of time it takes to cook will depend on the depth of your mixture in the internal tin, as well as the heat of your coals, but begin checking somewhere after 15-20 minutes. When cooked your bread should be golden on top and make a hollow sound when you tap it.

Damper

INGREDIENTS:

- 2 cups of Self Raising flour
- Enough milk to make a sticky dough
- 2 tablespoons of butter or margarine
- A good shake of salt

METHOD:

1. Mix the dry ingredients and rub the butter into the flour until it resembles bread crumbs.
2. Make a well in the centre and add the milk. Add just enough milk to make a sticky dough.
3. With floured hands, shape the damper and place in your lined camp oven. Using a trivet can help to stop the bottom from burning. Place the lid on securely and shovel a small amount of coals on top.
4. Cook on a bed of coals until the damper sounds hollow to tap.

Ideally make your damper wider rather than higher as it will cook more quickly. Add whatever takes your fancy to the basic ingredients – diced bacon and cheese is a delicious combination. For damper on a stick, simply wrap pieces of the damper around a clean (and non-poisonous) stick and rotate over the coals.

Apple Fritters

This recipe is very successful using bananas or pineapple rings too and is my favourite camp fire dessert. I usually mix up a brew in the afternoon and place my apple rounds in there so they are ready to just throw on the hot plate and cook. The fritters need to be used on the same day since the batter doesn't keep well.

INGREDIENTS:

- 1 cup of Self Raising flour
- 1 egg, lightly beaten
- Small squirt of vanilla essence
- 1 cup of milk
- 1 tablespoon of sugar
- 2 teaspoons of lemon juice
- Pinch salt
- Fruit such as apples, bananas, pineapple etc

METHOD:

1. Peel and core apples and slice into 4 mm round pieces.
2. Place the flour in a bowl and make a well in the centre.
3. Pour in the vanilla essence, beaten egg and milk and mix well, making sure there are no lumps.
4. Coat both sides of the fruit and fry in oil (or on an oiled BBQ plate) over a medium heat. Turn when small bubbles appear on top.
5. Serve with an extra squeeze of lemon and a sprinkle of sugar. Yum!

Big A*se Golden Syrup Dumplings

I can feel my a*se getting bigger with every mouthful, but Maria's dumplings are truly something to die for. Definitely be prepared for some vigorous exercise and a good round with the toothbrush after. This recipe feeds 10-12 people and is delicious served with fresh cream and custard. Preferably not the out-of-date long life custard we used, but what the heck, we survived!

DUMPLING INGREDIENTS:

- 2½ cups of Self Raising flour
- 100 grams of butter, melted
- 1 cup of sugar, preferably brown
- 1 cup of milk (or enough to make a thick mix)

SAUCE INGREDIENTS:

- 100 grams of butter
- 4½ cups of water
- 1½ cups of golden syrup
- 2 cups of brown sugar

METHOD:

1. To prepare the dumplings, melt the butter and then add the milk, the sugar and other dry ingredients. Mix well and set aside.
2. Place the syrup ingredients in a large camp oven over low heat coals (or on the hot plate). Bring slowly to the boil, stirring often to avoid it burning on the bottom.
3. When the syrup is bubbling, carefully place large dessertspoons full of the dumpling mixture into the sauce (I mould it a little with my hands) allowing a couple of seconds between each. Cover with the lid.
4. Begin checking around the 12-15 minute mark. You will know when they are cooked as they will be 'cake like' inside. Enjoy!

Lemonade Scones - Camp Oven Style

INGREDIENTS:

- 3 cups of Self Raising flour
- 1 cup of cream
- Just over 1 cup of Lemonade (the rest is for the cook)

METHOD:

1. Ensure you have a good bed of mature hot coals for cooking.
2. As with normal scones, place the flour in a bowl.
3. Make a well in the centre and add the cream and Lemonade.
4. Stir thoroughly with a flat bladed knife until just combined. The mixture should still be a little sticky. If it looks too sticky add a little more flour or more Lemonade if it seems too dry.
5. Sprinkle a little extra flour over a clean surface and tip mixture out.
6. With floured hands, gently pat until it is about 4 cm high all over.
7. Use a knife, or the rim of a cup to cut out the scones to the desired size and shape.
8. Place scones evenly around a well-oiled or floured tin that will fit inside your camp oven.
9. Use a small wire rack (or trivet) or an inverted (upside down) metal plate between your tin and the camp oven to keep the scones off the base of the dish. This will stop them from burning to a crisp on the bottom. Attach the lid securely.
10. Take a shovel-full of coals from the fire and sit your camp oven directly into the coal pit. Carefully place some shovelled coals on top of the camp oven.
11. Cook for approximately 10 minutes or until the scones are golden on top and cooked through. Now get out the jar of jam, some extra cream and go to town.

The Meaty Bits

An everyday guide to cooking with meat

A Butcher's Guide to Choosing Your Meat

Let's take a butcher's look at some of the more common cuts of meat that you will find on the supermarket shelf. As a general rule, when it comes to beef, a marbling pattern of fat running through your meat is a good thing, as it will ensure a nice tender steak at the end.

RUMP
Rump is probably the most common and versatile cut on the market. In the medium price range it has a wide range of uses, holds good flavour and marinates well.

SCOTCH FILLET
This is the cut that you see on restaurant menus with the bacon wrapped around it. It is a delicious piece of meat and is best served medium.

T-BONE
As the name suggests, a T-shaped bone runs through the centre of this steak. Popular on the BBQ or grill, it can be easy to overcook due to the smaller portion of meat on one side. Best under-done.

SIRLOIN
This is the large side of the T-bone steak and is best grilled over a high heat and rested as it does not contain a lot of fat.

BLADE
This cut of meat is most commonly used for braising or stewing as it can be quite tough. For this reason it is best cooked slowly over a medium to low heat for several hours. Though not the most tender cut of meat, it has great flavours. Chuck steak also falls into this category.

SHANKS
To think I used to give these to the dog! These are absolutely delicious if quickly braised over a high heat and then slow cooked on a low heat for several hours with some onion, fresh herbs, red wine, beef stock and whatever else takes your fancy.

The Meaty Bits

Is there such a thing as the perfect steak every time?

This is a difficult question as it relies heavily on three things – a good cut of meat, the correct cooking technique, and the preferences of the diner.

I am not afraid to admit that I am a bit hit and miss when it comes to cooking a successful steak as I tend to panic that it will be undercooked, overcooked, or not even cooked. And how it's cooked of course, is completely dependent on how your guests like their steak. All this scares the beejeebers out of me.

So this next bit is dedicated to all those, such as myself, who struggle a bit in this department. In order to get the right advice I headed straight to Roy our local butcher as I was not prepared to put my head on the chopping block alone!

A Guide to Cooking Steak

- Obviously your first decision is the cut of meat you choose for the job (see previous information). Heat your pan or hot plate to a fairly high heat and then quickly sear your steak for a minute or so on both sides. This means a short time on each side just until you get some nice colouring happening.
- (As a guide for a medium steak) – then continue to cook for 4 minutes either side and then remove to 'rest' for 4-5 minutes before serving.
- Someone once told me that meat should 'rest' for half the length of its cooking time eg if cooked for 10 minutes, it should 'rest' for 5.

Roy's Finger Test

Now take this as you will, but there is a science in determining how well your steak is cooked, and it's all in the fingering.

To do this, simply make a circle using your thumb and forefinger. Make sure your fingers stay loose. Now use the forefinger on your other hand to gently push on the meaty part just up from the base of your thumb. In theory, this is meant to simulate the density and feel of the differently cooked pieces of meat.

FIGURE 1: Rare – forefinger

FIGURE 2: Medium Rare – second finger

FIGURE 3: Medium – ring finger

FIGURE 4: Well Done – little finger

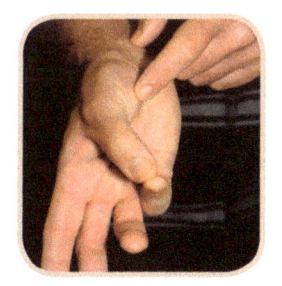

The Meaty Bits

A Guide to Marinating

There are two main reasons why we marinate things such as meat - firstly to tenderise them and secondly, to enhance their taste and flavour.

Liquids such as lemon juice, vinegar, yogurt and wine are naturally acidic and help to tenderise the meat by breaking down its fibres, so most recipes contain at least one of these ingredients.

Meat needs time to absorb the marinade and this time varies depending on the cut. For example, cubes of meat for kebabs will need around 3 hours while other cuts can sit covered in the fridge, anywhere from 12-24 hours. It's always a good idea to turn or toss your meat in the marinade from time to time to make sure the flavour is evenly distributed.

One word of warning; although you may like to baste your meat with the leftover marinade while it's cooking, never pour it over the finished product or it could make you crook.

Here are some easy marinating ideas with ingredients you will most likely have at home already – especially some of those fresh herbs you've grown.

Chicken Marinades

Teriyaki Marinade (GF)

INGREDIENTS:

- A small cup of water
- A small cup of soy sauce (Tamari is the name given to gluten free soy sauce)
- ¾ cup of white sugar
- 3 tablespoons of white vinegar
- 3 tablespoons of gluten free Worcestershire sauce
- 3 tablespoons of vegetable oil
- 1 teaspoon of freshly grated ginger – or ½ teaspoon of dry
- 1 clove of freshly pressed garlic – or 1 teaspoon of granulated
- ¼ white onion, peeled and very finely diced – or 1 teaspoon of dried onion flakes

Asian Satay Sauce (GF)

This makes about a cup of marinade, adjust the quantities as necessary. This sauce is delicious on chicken skewers and is best left to marinate overnight.

INGREDIENTS:

- ¼ cup of Asian rice wine vinegar – or just use white vinegar if that's all you have
- ¼ cup of light soy sauce (Tamari is the name given to gluten free soy sauce)
- ¼ cup of nutty peanut butter
- A squeeze of lemon juice
- 1 tablespoon of honey
- 1 tablespoon of sesame oil
- A little grated fresh ginger
- Some finely chopped coriander

Orange and Tarragon Marinade

This is delicious with chicken. Place your chicken portions in with the marinade and refrigerate overnight. Remove chicken with tongs and fry lightly till golden on both sides. Place chicken in a single layer in a baking dish and pour over marinade. Cover with foil and cook for 1 hour in a 180°C oven.

INGREDIENTS:

- ¼ cup of French Tarragon, roughly chopped and tightly packed
- 4 decent sprigs of lemon thyme, stripped
- ¼ cup of balsamic vinegar
- ¼ cup of golden syrup (check label for a gluten free guest as it may contain sugar derived from wheat)
- Zest and juice of 1 orange
- Zest and juice of 1 lemon
- 2 cloves of garlic, peeled and segmented
- The flesh segments of 2 whole oranges
- Salt and pepper

Pork Marinades

Honey Mustard Marinade with a Tarragon Twist (GF)

This recipe has a distinctively French feel to it, especially with the tarragon. If you've never tried tarragon, it's definitely worth a go – but don't be tempted to use too much as it is quite a strong herb and can easily overpower a dish.

INGREDIENTS:

- 3 tablespoons of soy sauce (Tamari is the name given to gluten free soy sauce)
- 2 tablespoons of vegetable oil
- 3 tablespoons of Dijon mustard
- 2 teaspoons of honey
- 2 tablespoons of finely chopped fresh French tarragon
- 3 large cloves of garlic, peeled and crushed
- A good grind of black pepper

Plum Sauce

This is terrific on spare ribs but would also be nice with pork chops or as baste for a roast.

INGREDIENTS:

- Your favourite plum sauce – it could be Grandma's homemade stuff or why not try a spicy Asian variety from the shop (check ingredients for a gluten free guest)
- Chinese five spice powder

METHOD:

1. Simply use the desired amount of plum sauce and add a light sprinkle of the five spice powder to it. Stir well and coat your meat, marinating for at least 5 hours or overnight if possible.

Beef Marinades

Basic Red Wine Marinade (GF)

INGREDIENTS:

- Approximately ½ cup of last night's leftover red wine (if you are a coeliac, be wary)
- A splash of vegetable oil
- A splash of soy sauce (Tamari is the name given to gluten free soy sauce)
- 2 cloves of garlic, peeled and crushed
- 2 tablespoons of gluten free Worcestershire sauce
- 2 tablespoons of tomato sauce
- 2 teaspoons of brown sugar

Beef 'N' Beer Marinade

INGREDIENTS:

- ⅓ of a can of your favourite beer – I'm sure you won't need convincing to drink the rest
- 1 tablespoon of honey
- A good grind of black pepper
- A grind of salt
- 1 teaspoon of dried mustard powder – or 2 teaspoons of your favourite mustard paste – French, wholegrain etc
- 2 tablespoons of brown sugar or golden syrup

METHOD:

1. Place all ingredients, except the beer, in a microwave safe jug or dish and heat on HIGH for a minute or so until honey and sugar have melted and dissolved.
2. Allow to cool.
3. Add the beer and stir well.
4. Add the meat, and allow to marinate for a minimum of 2-3 hours, turning half way through.
5. Drain well and then throw your steak on a nice hot BBQ.

Lamb Marinades

Jam and Yogurt Marinade (GF)

This is very tasty on pork or chicken and is an example of how yogurt is used to tenderise meat. Allow a minimum of 4–6 hours to marinate. Nice on kebabs.

INGREDIENTS:

- ½ cup of natural Greek style Yogurt
- 1 small onion, peeled and very finely diced
- 2 tablespoons of apricot jam
- 1½ tablespoons of freshly chopped mint
- ½ teaspoon of cinnamon powder
- ¼ teaspoon of ground ginger
- 1 clove of garlic, peeled and crushed

Sweet Chilli Rub

As the name suggests this marinade is best rubbed into the meat and left for 4-6 hours or overnight - delicious on the BBQ.

INGREDIENTS:

- 1 dessertspoon of grainy mustard paste (can buy gluten free varieties)
- The grated rind of one lemon and a small squeeze of juice
- 2 dessertspoons of honey, melted in the microwave if necessary
- 1 large clove of garlic, peeled and crushed – or ½ teaspoon of granulated garlic
- 1 slightly rounded teaspoon of curry powder
- 1 teaspoon of turmeric powder (an orange coloured spice)
- 1 teaspoon of Sambal Olek (a spicy Indonesian paste) – you could also use sweet chilli sauce as a less spicy option (can buy gluten free varieties)

Meaty Recipes

At this present time, lamb is an expensive commodity but as most people living on the land know, the value of our product can take a dive at any time. For that reason, many farming families have become very creative with the ways in which they have used lamb over the years, and I often substituted it for beef when times were tough.

Lili's Lamb Parmi

Of course you will notice that this dish is made in exactly the same way as a normal Parmi, but with lamb. You can do the same with chicken breasts by slicing them horizontally, pounding them and crumbing in the same manner.

INGREDIENTS:

- 6-8 large loin chops, meat removed from the bones
- 2-3 cups of fresh bread crumbs
- ½ cup of grated Parmesan cheese
- 1 dessertspoon of dry Italian herbs (or a combination of fresh oregano, rosemary, garlic and parsley)
- Salt and pepper
- 2 eggs, whisked
- ½ cup of milk
- 1 cup of Plain flour
- A jar of pre-prepared pasta sauce (or make your own)
- A good handful of grated cheese
- Some vegetable oil for frying – about 2 tablespoons (may need to add more)

METHOD:

1. Preheat the oven to 180°C.
2. Place each piece of meat between some plastic wrap, one at a time and pound with a meat mallet until nice and thin. Repeat with remaining meat.
3. Place the flour on a plate.
4. Combine the eggs and milk on another plate.
5. Place the bread crumbs, Parmesan cheese, herbs, salt and pepper on a third plate and combine well.
6. Now, starting with the flour, carefully coat each piece of meat, moving on to the egg mixture and then finally the crumbs.
7. Heat the oil in a frying pan and cook the meat until golden on both sides, over a medium heat. Repeat with the rest of the meat, adding more oil if the pan becomes dry. Remove and drain on paper towel.
8. Arrange the meat in a single layer in a large oven proof baking dish or tray.
9. Pour over the pasta sauce and then sprinkle with grated cheese. Cover with foil, (shiny side towards the food).
10. Cook in the preheated 180°C oven for approximately 20 minutes, or until the meat is properly heated through and the cheese is melted. Remove the foil for the last few minutes of cooking.
11. Serve with some mashed potatoes and winter vegetables or a fresh garden salad.

Lozza's Lamb Chops with Fancy Sauce (GF)

Now it doesn't get too much easier than this quick and tasty meal – and you won't want to share it either. It works really well with leftover BBQ lamb chops (as lamb goes really well with mint) or with sausages that are already cooked – not so good with steak but hey! I suggest you get a pot of potatoes on to boil ready to mash and some accompanying vegetables for when this dish is ready to serve. And don't forget the bread and butter to mop up the Fancy Sauce.

INGREDIENTS:

- The desired number of lamb chops of your choice, let's say 8
- 1 x 420 gram can of gluten free tomato soup
- Equivalent to half the can of water
- 1 onion, peeled and finely diced
- 1 level dessertspoon of curry powder
- A handful of fresh mint (from your herb garden) or 1 teaspoon of dried mint
- Salt and pepper
- 1 tablespoon of oil for frying

METHOD:

1. Preheat your oven to 180°C.
2. If your chops (or sausages) are not already cooked, either fry them in a pan with the oil or cook them under the griller. Drain well.
3. If you used a frying pan, add the diced onion (and a little more oil if needed) and cook until the onion is golden.
4. Add the curry powder and stir for a minute or so.
5. Add the soup, water, salt, pepper and mint and bring to the boil.
6. Arrange the cooked chops (or sausages) in a single layer in a large baking dish. I advise to give it a spray with cooking oil first to make cleaning easier.
7. Pour over the tomato mixture and cover with foil, shiny side towards the meat.
8. Cook for 25-30 minutes in the preheated oven, or until chops are tender.
9. Scatter with some extra mint and serve with your favourite veggies.

The Meaty Bits

Slow Cooked Moroccan Lamb (GF)

As the name implies, this recipe works best if you own (or can borrow) a slow cooker. This way it cooks on a low heat for many hours, ensuring you end up with tender, juicy lamb. If you don't have a slow cooker, you could put it in a large casserole dish that has a lid. Simply place it in the oven on 150°C for a good 4-5 hours, until the meat is very tender.

With the addition of the apricots, this is a deliciously sweet dish best served with a plain couscous or rice. If you have a gluten free guest, use rice or quinoa instead of the couscous. For an extra treat you can add some flaked almonds when serving.

INGREDIENTS:

- Approximately 1 kg of diced, lean lamb
- 1 large brown onion, peeled and diced
- 2 teaspoons of minced garlic
- ½ cup of water
- ½ cup of orange juice
- 1 small gluten free beef stock cube (or ½ a large one)
- 2 tablespoons of honey
- 1 teaspoon of ground cinnamon
- Either a handful of diced dried apricots or ½ cup of preserved apricots – juice drained
- 1 teaspoon of dried ginger, or 2 teaspoons of grated fresh ginger
- 1 large teaspoon of salt
- A small squeeze of lemon juice
- Some freshly ground black pepper
- Fresh coriander for serving
- Natural yogurt for serving
- Flaked almonds for serving, optional

METHOD:

1. Place all ingredients in the slow cooker, except for the coriander and yogurt.
2. Cook on LOW for 5-6 hours and serve topped with the yogurt, almonds and coriander.

84   The Meaty Bits

Lisa's Hurry Curry with Rice (GF)

This makes a lovely sweet curry that's kind on the rear end. Just be cautious what brand of chutney you are using for the gluten free guest.

INGREDIENTS:

- 1 x 500 gram packet of beef mince
- 1 small onion, peeled and diced
- 1 level dessertspoon of curry powder, or more if you're game
- 1 sweet apple, peeled and diced
- 1 banana, peeled and sliced
- 2 tablespoons of gluten free chutney or tomato paste (if you don't have chutney you could replace with sugar for a little sweetness)
- 2 tablespoons of desiccated coconut
- A good handful of sultanas
- 1 x 800 gram tin of puréed or diced tomatoes
- 1- 2 gluten free beef stock cubes, crumbled
- 1 tablespoon of oil
- 1 quantity of rice (see Fail-Safe Rice recipe)

METHOD:

1. Fry the mince and onion in the oil until golden.
2. Add the curry powder and stir around for a minute or so.
3. Add the remaining ingredients and bring to the boil.
4. Reduce the heat and simmer (with a lid half on) for 12-15 minutes. Serve with rice.

Note: You can make fancy rice shapes using decorative lids or bowls. Simply oil the inside well and pack the rice firmly in. Then just carefully tip it out onto your serving plate.

The Meaty Bits

Quick Chick Curry (GF) (with an optional Indian twist)

I have experimented substituting normal dry curry powder (which results in a yellowish curry) for Tandoori paste in this recipe with tasty Indian style results. Although it ends up being an unusual pinkish curry, it's delicious with a dollop of natural yogurt and a sprinkling of fresh coriander on top. Your choice - yellow or pink.

INGREDIENTS:

- 1 tablespoon of oil
- 1 onion, peeled and either sliced or diced
- ¼ of a head of cauliflower, cut into small flowerets
- 1 medium capsicum, deseeded and either sliced or diced
- 1 tablespoon of dry curry powder (or 2 tablespoons of gluten free Tandoori paste for an Indian twist)
- 1 apple, peeled and diced
- 2 cups of water
- 1 gluten free chicken stock cube, crumbled (or 500 mls of liquid gluten free stock)
- A good tablespoon of your favourite pickles, optional (check if gluten free)
- Approximately ½ a cooked chicken, shredded (I try to think of my hips and remove the skin first). If you don't have pre-cooked chicken, you can simply fry it up with the onion and capsicum.
- Natural yogurt and coriander for serving if using the Tandoori paste

METHOD:

1. Heat oil in a frying pan and add the onion and capsicum. Fry for 3-4 minutes or until onion is transparent.
2. Add the diced apple and continue to fry for another 1-2 minutes.
3. Add the curry powder (or Tandoori paste) and stir well for another minute.
4. Add the water, stock cube, pickles and shredded chicken and bring back to the boil (big bubbles).
5. Reduce the heat and simmer (small bubbles) for 15 minutes. If you feel it needs thickening, combine 1 teaspoon of Cornflour with 2 dessertspoons of water and mix into a paste. Stir into the curry until it thickens. Make sure you don't use Cornflour for your gluten free guest though.

The Meaty Bits

The Art of Preserving

Making nature's finest last all year round

Preserving has no doubt been around since fruit and vegetables came into existence but even if you don't have a garden or fruit trees yourself, all is not lost. Hit up Grandma, friends, relatives or raid random trees on the sides of country roads to preserve your own little piece of Nature. Another good trick is to get friendly with your local grocers as they often have produce, which is a little past saleable, going out cheap. This is still fine for jams and chutneys and if you don't have time to make it up straight away, just cut them up and freeze them for a later date.

But first, some basic guidelines on preserving fruits and jams. It can be done easily at home without having to purchase expensive equipment and specialised jars.

Sterilising Jam Jars and Metal Lids

It is absolutely paramount (very, very important) that your bottling jars are well sterilised. It is also very important that once they are sterilised, you don't touch the inside area of the jars or lids with your fingers, as this will add bacteria which will cause mould down the track.

THERE ARE SEVERAL METHODS OF STERILISING BUT THIS IS THE ONE I USE:

1. Remove any labels and glue (read on for tips).
2. Ensure that none of your jars have cracks or chips and that you have the correct lid for the jar.
3. Wash the jars (and lids) very well in hot soapy water.
4. Rinse them with clean water to remove any trace of detergent and then place them in the oven on their sides (and face lids upwards like a cup). I like to put my lids on the top shelf as if the lids are under the jars you run the risk of cruddy oven bits falling off into your sterilised lids when you are removing the jars.
5. Heat the oven to 120°C and leave them in there for at least 20 minutes. Note that your oven should be cold when you put the jars in.
6. Turn off the oven and leave them to cool slightly before bottling. Note that you should never attempt to pour boiling hot fruit into a cold jar or you are asking for trouble. I always leave my jars and lids in the warm oven until I am ready to bottle. I figure they are sterile while they are in there and bringing them out into the air is just another opportunity for germs to get in.

WHEN IT COMES TO SEALING THE JARS, THERE ARE TWO OPTIONS:

1. You can re-use the lids from jars such as pickles that have a line of gum inside and the 'pop' top, provided the seals (and jars) are in excellent condition. Otherwise you can buy new ones from most food warehouses. Always double check that your lid is screwed on tightly before your produce cools.

   OR

2. You can buy clear cellophane jam seals in packets at the supermarket. Follow the sealing directions on the packet.

In the packet you will find cellophane covers, rubber bands and labels. The instructions are all there for you but if I am bottling chutneys, I always moisten the cellophane with vinegar (which is a natural preservative) instead of water. I never use my fingers to moisten the covers as this could add bacteria. I do this by pouring a little vinegar onto a small plate and then laying the cover in the vinegar. Then place it over your jar, vinegar side towards the chutney, and then carefully secure the rubber band. Pull the cellophane gently into place but don't pull it too tight as it will naturally tighten as it cools. Having said that I prefer to always use metal lids where possible as there is less long-term shrinkage.

I use water, as suggested on the packet, when using cellophane covers for sealing sweet jams.

Note: *Without a doubt the most laborious part of re-using jars is the removal of the commercial label – some just seem to come off easier than others. I have had the most success doing the following:*

1. Firstly, if you are really, really lucky it may be one of those easy off labels. Always have a go at getting the label off the dry jar first as you might get lucky!
2. Soak jars in a sink full of cold water and some methylated spirits at least overnight. Using cold water seems to get you in less of a sticky mess with the glue on the jars.
3. Scratch or peel off what you can using a flat bladed, flexible butter knife.
4. Use a scourer and hot, soapy water to remove the last bits of glue if you were not completely successful with the knife. A little extra metho may also be required. Rinse very well in soapy, then clean water. Good luck.

My Aunty G swears by using a piece of paper towel with Eucalyptus oil on it to remove the glue once you have scraped the labels off. Worth a try if you have some on hand, but remember to rinse them well afterwards.

General Preserving and Jam Making Tips:

- Any foaminess should be scooped off the top of your jam during the boiling process. Some fruits, such as strawberries, create more foam than others so I usually do this each time I stir in the early stages of the cooking.

- If you smell your produce starting to burn, it may still be possible to salvage it. DO NOT loosen the bottom of the pan as this will incorporate all the burnt stuff into your mixture. Carefully pour the good layer of jam or chutney into a clean saucepan. Then, if it still smells burnt, you probably need to start again. If not, continue to boil until ready to bottle.

- Lemon juice is added to jams to help them set as it is both acidic and high in pectin. Pectin is a natural carbohydrate which is present in fruits. Some fruits have a higher pectin level than others. Those high in pectin include apples, quinces, citrus and some plums, whilst strawberries, apricots, peaches, pineapples, blueberries and cherries for example are quite low in pectin. Lemon juice aids the pectin level and also helps to stop bacteria from forming. I always use freshly squeezed lemon and would only use bottled lemon juice as an absolute last resort. You can also buy commercial jam setters.

- Jams and jellies require a combination of sugar, acid and pectin to set. Chutneys and relishes often have Cornflour added near the end of the cooking process to thicken them up a bit if necessary.

The Art of Preserving

- How do you know when to bottle? There is no exact time that it takes for a jam to reach setting point, but there are ways to test to see if it is ready. Firstly you should notice after some time that the mixture is beginning to thicken and may turn slightly darker, with the bubbles becoming more lava like. To double check, put a clean plate in the freezer for a few minutes. Now place a small spoonful of jam onto the cold plate and let it sit for a few seconds. If you try to drag a spoon through the mixture it should leave a clear line and not be runny. If your jam is not setting, you could try adding a small amount of extra sugar and another squeeze of lemon juice. Continue to boil and see if further thickening takes place.

- When bottling, I find it much easier if I line up my jars in a row. This means that when I am pouring, any spillage won't get on the other jars. This saves time and mess cleaning up. If you do get spillage on the outside of your jars (especially near the lid) make sure you wipe it up with a clean piece of paper towel, otherwise it will encourage mould to creep into your jar.

- Always fill jars as close as you can to the top, without the possibility of it spilling over – the less air space, the less chance of bacteria. Any half-filled bottles of jam or chutney should be refrigerated and used first.

- After filling your jars and attaching the 'pop-top' metal lids, it is normal to hear a popping sound some time later. This is the jar vacuum sealing itself and is a sound you want to hear. Once sealed properly the middle of the lid should be depressed like they are when you buy them in the shop.

- Storage is the key to longevity (keeping a long time). For lasting results, store your jams and preserves in a cool, dark place. Excessive light can cause fruit to discolour and may result in the shrinkage or drying up of preserves and jams. I find there is a lot less chance of shrinkage using metal lids as opposed to clear preserve seals.

- If your jams or chutneys seem too dry, they can still be salvaged in the short term. If I've cracked the lid and it looks a bit dried up I boil the kettle and add a tablespoon of hot water. In addition I might whack it in the microwave on HIGH for 30 seconds or so and then give it a good stir to help it reconstitute. Following this you will need to keep it in the fridge for use in the not too distant future.

- Your best chance of success is to use a recipe which has been tried and tested, as messing around with amounts and ingredients can have unreliable results. Resist the urge to double or triple the recipe; instead put two or three saucepans of the same recipe on at a time, as large amounts can take a long time to set, especially when making jams.

- Finally – never make or bottle your jams and chutneys wearing thongs. I made this mistake once, with painful results!

Strawberry and Pineapple Jam (GF)

I had some strawberries and pineapple left over from a fruit platter so decided to cut them up and turn them into some jam. Waste not, want not I say. This recipe makes a small quantity, only yielding about two large jars of jam.

INGREDIENTS:

- 900 grams of diced strawberries and finely diced pineapple (about 450 grams of each)
- 600 grams of sugar (cane sugar is gluten free)
- The juice of one lemon

METHOD:

1. Place fruit, sugar and lemon juice into a saucepan that's about half the size again of your mixture. Stir with a wooden spoon to incorporate the mixture.
2. Bring slowly to the boil and continue to simmer for approximately 1 hour, stirring often.
3. Each time you stir, skim off any foam with a clean spoon.
4. When your jam is at setting point (see instructions) carefully pour into hot, sterilised jars and seal.
5. Store in a cool, dark place.

Sweet Mango Chutney (GF)

Although mangoes are not native to my neck of the woods I always like to take advantage of buying them on sale because I just loooove mango chutney. You might be lucky enough to have some growing in your own back yard but I will often buy mangoes when they are going out cheap, scoop out the flesh and freeze them until I have time to make my chutney. This recipe makes just over 2.5 kg of chutney (about 6 medium coffee jars).

INGREDIENTS:

- The flesh from 6 large, ripe mangoes (1.5 kilograms of flesh)
- 230 grams of brown onions, peeled and roughly chopped (throw them in the food processor to save the tears)
- 1 cup of raisins
- 500 mls (2 cups) of white vinegar
- 750 grams (just under 4 cups) of white sugar (cane sugar is gluten free)
- 1 tablespoon of salt
- 1 teaspoon of mustard seeds
- 1 teaspoon of ground nutmeg
- 1 teaspoon of mixed spice
- 1 teaspoon of curry powder
- A good pinch of ground cloves
- Sterilised jars (not an ingredient as such)

METHOD:

1. Place all ingredients into a large, wide, deep saucepan.
2. Stir ingredients well with a long handled wooden spoon. Turn on to a medium heat and bring it to a rolling boil (big bubbles).
3. Reduce and simmer (small bubbles) for approximately 30-45 minutes, stirring with a wooden spoon on regular occasions to prevent burning and sticking. If you have a timer I suggest you set it at 10-minute intervals. At this point you may also like to use your potato masher to break up the mangoes a bit or purée it with a hand blender if you want it super smooth – but, take great care not to burn yourself in the process.
4. Whilst the chutney is simmering, sterilise your jars (see previous instructions).
5. When the chutney has reduced, thickened slightly and turned a darker colour, you are ready to bottle. Using tongs or pot holders, carefully remove the jars and lids from the oven and set out on the bench.
6. Use a ladle or heat-proof jug to transfer the hot chutney into the jars and then seal immediately, making sure you observe the sterilisation principles. A clean tea towel or kitchen gloves can help if using screw top jars.
7. Allow to sit until cool, then label and store in a cool, dark place. Will keep indefinitely.

Zucchini and Apple Relish (GF)

When you grow zucchinis you have to become very creative in the ways you use them, because you are likely to harvest them in wheelbarrow loads. This relish is not only delicious, with a touch of spice, but also makes a great gift when bottled up for the festive season. Recipe makes approximately 2.5 kgs of relish.

INGREDIENTS:

- 1 kg of zucchini flesh (unpeeled, any pithy seeds removed and chopped into large chunks)
- 500 grams (roughly 4 large) brown onions, peeled and quartered
- 500 grams of apples (roughly 5-6 medium apples – or you could substitute pears or a combination of the two) peeled, deseeded and quartered
- 250 grams of red capsicum (roughly 2 large) deseeded and quartered (you can use green as well)
- 1 red chilli, deseeded
- 500 mls (2 cups) of white vinegar
- 700 grams (3½ cups) of sugar (cane sugar is gluten free)
- 1 tablespoon of turmeric
- 1 dessertspoon of curry powder
- 1 tablespoon of salt
- 1 tablespoon of brown or yellow mustard seeds (or you could use a gluten free wholegrain mustard spread)
- ½ teaspoon of cayenne pepper
- 1 tablespoon of Cornflour stirred into 2 tablespoons of vinegar, extra – optional
  Note: You can buy gluten free Cornflour or simply leave it out.
- Sterilised jars and lids or seals

METHOD:

1. Dice all the vegetables and fruit in your food processor in batches. If you don't have a food processor you'll need a lot of patience or you could use a hand blender at the end. Don't over-process as it will end up looking like mash and you will lose all the nice colours in the relish.
2. Place vegetables, sugar and fruit in a large saucepan and slowly bring to the boil. I do this with the lid half on. Reduce the heat and simmer for approximately 30 minutes (adding a touch of water if it seems too dry) or until the vegetables are soft. Remember to stir every now and then.
3. Add the vinegar, salt and spices and bring back to the boil. Continue to stir often while simmering (small bubbles) for a further 10-15 minutes.
4. Pour in the combined extra vinegar and Cornflour and stir well until thickened. If I think the relish is thick enough already, I don't always add the Cornflour.
5. Bottle into warm sterilised jars and seal immediately. I like to use metal lids for chutneys and relishes as they can be quite prone to shrinkage over a longer period of time if you use plastic seals.

The Art of Preserving

Quintessential Quince Paste (GF)

I always thought quinces were one of those nothing fruits that nobody liked as they are pretty bland in flavour; that was until I discovered quince paste. I am no longer satisfied to see unwanted quinces rotting away under the tree. I could never palate blue cheese until I discovered that it is a match made in heaven with quince paste – now I have to restrain myself.

Yes, making quince paste is a bit time consuming and laborious (and you definitely need a kitchen timer on hand) but OMG – the results will have you enjoying the fruits of your labour all year round.

INGREDIENTS:

- 10 large quinces, carefully peeled, cored and roughly chopped with all seeds (and any bad bits) removed
- 3-4 extra quinces, peeled and roughly chopped but with the cores and seeds left in
- 2 cups of water
- The juice of two large lemons
- Sugar – see directions below (cane sugar is gluten free)

METHOD:

1. Place all of the quinces, water and lemon juice into the large, deep saucepan and bring to the boil (big bubbles). I leave the lid partially on.
2. Reduce the heat and simmer (small bubbles) for 30-40 minutes or until the fruit is soft, stirring every 5 or so minutes (hence the timer).
3. Allow to cool slightly then either purée in batches using the food processor (the cheats' method that I use which seems to mash everything up nicely) or you can pass it quite laboriously through the mouli sieve, discarding all the seeds and skins. This effort will result in a lovely clear paste.
4. At this point you need to weigh your cooked quince and then return it to the saucepan.
5. Add in three quarters of the quinces' weight in sugar. This means that if your quinces weigh 2 kg, you need to add 1.5 kg of sugar. At this point you need to be sure that your quince mixture takes up no more than a quarter of the height of your saucepan to allow for when it turns into Mt Vesuvius!
6. Stir well and turn on to a medium heat, still with the lid partially on. The lid will also act as a human shield when stirring. Bring the mixture back to a simmer for between 2–3 hours – YES hours. Now here's the bit where you must dedicate yourself solely to the task as it will need a light stir every 3-4 minutes. I always set the timer as it is infuriating to get this far and then stuff it up by burning it. Make sure you use the wooden spoon to move across the bottom of the saucepan thoroughly and loosen any sticky patches. If the bottom does get burnt, you can either transfer it to another saucepan (being careful not to dislodge the burnt stuff) or if it is near the end of the cooking – remove the good paste and spread onto your tray. I know you may be reading this and at this point are thinking "Can't be stuffed", but trust me – it's worth it! Take great care when stirring, especially towards the end when it starts to thicken. I sometimes wear an oven mitt or wrap my arm in an old tea towel, as it is like molten lava. Eventually your paste will become quite thick and dark and when you move your spoon through the saucepan, it will leave a track. You can now remove it from the heat and are off the hook with time for a quick coldie while it cools slightly.
7. Carefully pour the paste into two lined biscuit trays (that have 1.5 cm sides) or use lamington or Swiss roll tins. The paste should be spread evenly about 1–1.5 cm thick.
8. The final process is the drying, at which point you have some choices. If you want the quicker method you can place your trays in the oven with only the fan running (no temperature) overnight or until the paste is completely set. You can also air dry it by leaving it covered on your kitchen bench with a mesh cloth, which is propped up so it is not touching the paste (to stop flies and insects) or I have even heard of people putting it in a sunny place such as the back parcel tray of the car. Air-drying will take between 2-4 days. You will know when it's ready because when you slice the paste it will be set all the way through and not sticky on the bottom.

9. Cut it into the desired sized squares and wrap firstly in greaseproof paper, then foil, and then finally store in an airtight container in a cool, dark place.
10. Now go out and buy the blue cheese and crack a bottle of your favourite wine and celebrate all your good work.

Lisa's Sweet Pickles (GF)

Cauliflowers are one of the easiest vegetables to grow and when you do, you usually end up with a lot of them. There are lots of pickle recipes which are much quicker, but I love the taste of this one – it tastes loads better than the pickles you buy in the shops.

INGREDIENTS:

- 1 large cauliflower, cut into small flowerets (little flowers) stems included
- 8 large brown onions, peeled and either sliced or diced (though I am lazy and buzz batches for a few seconds each in my food processor)
- 1½ tablespoons of salt - (I use the cheap cooking salt)
- 2 cups water
- 6 cups white vinegar
- 2 cups sugar
- ½ cup Plain flour (leave out for a gluten free option)
- 2 tablespoons dry mustard powder (in the spice section at the shop)
- 1 tablespoon of yellow mustard seeds, optional (also in the spice section)
- 2 tablespoons of turmeric (in the same section)
- 1 finely diced red spur chilli (the long red ones) seeds removed
- Tissues or a handkerchief – you will need them for the onions but it will be worth it

METHOD:

1. Slice and cut the cauliflower into small pieces and place in a large bowl or vessel such as an empty ice cream bucket. There is quite a lot of vegetable.
2. Add the onions and diced chilli to the cauliflower. Sprinkle with the salt and give a light stir. Cover with plastic wrap (or place inside a large plastic bag or container with a lid) and let stand for several hours or, better still, overnight. If the weather is cool, it is fine to leave it out on the bench – otherwise put it in the fridge. I would advise using the large plastic container with a lid if you are putting it in the fridge to avoid the rest of your food tasting like onions.
3. The next day, drain the liquid and rinse ingredients lightly under cold running water and drain for a few moments in a colander. Place the vegetables in a large, heavy based saucepan.
4. Add one cup of the water, turmeric and mustard to the vegetable mixture with the vinegar and sugar etc.
5. Bring to the boil and then simmer for approximately one hour or until the vegetables are soft, stirring often. Combine the remaining water and flour and stir in until it thickens.
6. Sterilise your clean jars and lids (see detailed directions).
7. When the vegetables are soft you can choose to mash or purée the pickle mixture (if you like your relish smoother) just don't burn yourself in the process.
8. Using clean tongs, carefully remove the hot jars and lids, being careful not to contaminate them.
9. Allow the pickles to cool a little and then carefully pour into the hot sterilised jars. Make sure you wipe up any spills on the outside of the jars with some damp paper towel. Secure the lids tightly, label and store in a cool, dry place indefinitely. Try not to eat for at least three weeks to allow the flavour to mature.
10. This recipe makes approximately 3 kg of pickles which is about 6 large gherkin or onion jars.

The Art of Preserving

Ronda's Homemade Sauce (GF)

Ronda's famous sauce is a Smith family tradition and is simply too good not to share. Despite the fact that it has a long cooking time it may well be the best dead horse you've ever eaten. Recipe makes around 2 kg of sauce.

INGREDIENTS:

- 3.6 kg of tomatoes (preferably Romas), chopped
- 110 grams of salt
- 30 grams of garlic, peeled and crushed
  (or you can use 15 grams of granulated garlic)
- 950 mls of white vinegar
- 900 grams of sugar
- 30 grams of whole peppercorns
- 30 grams of whole cloves
- 30 grams of all spice
- ½ teaspoon of cayenne pepper
- Some calico cloth and non-plastic coated string

METHOD:

1. Place the chopped tomatoes, salt and garlic in a large bowl and stir well. Cover and let stand overnight. Drain well.
2. Cut a small square of calico cloth and enclose the peppercorns, cloves, all spice and cayenne pepper in the centre, then secure the bag tightly using the string. This can be squeezed out and frozen successfully afterwards to make one more batch of sauce.
3. Place the tomato mixture, vinegar, sugar and the spice bag in a large saucepan and stir lightly to combine. Bring to the boil.
4. Reduce the heat and simmer for a minimum of 5 hours, stirring often until the sauce has darkened and become thick with lava like bubbles.
5. Remove from the heat and put through a mouli sieve to remove any seeds and skins before bottling in sterilised jars. Ronda also tells me that she has bottled this sauce quite successfully when cold.

Pasta Sauce with Red Wine

If placed in sterilised jars, this pasta sauce can be kept for months in a cool, dark place. This recipe makes just over 2 litres, which is equivalent to 3 large pasta sauce jars. When adding to your favourite Italian dish, I often add a crumbled beef stock cube for some extra flavour.

INGREDIENTS:

- Approximately 2 kg of tomatoes, roughly chopped
- 3 onions, peeled and coarsely diced
- 6 cloves of garlic, peeled and crushed
- 6 dessertspoons of sugar
- ¾ cup of last night's red wine (check for gluten free people)
- 1 tablespoon of salt
- Several grinds of black pepper
- A large handful of fresh basil, finely chopped
- A smaller handful of fresh rosemary, finely chopped

METHOD:

1. Place the chopped tomatoes, onions and garlic in a large saucepan and bring to the boil. Reduce and simmer for approximately 20 minutes, or until tender. At this point you could pass the mixture through a mouli sieve to remove any seeds or skins from the mixture, though I am just happy to give it a buzz with my hand blender at the end as I don't mind it chunky.
2. Add the sugar, red wine, salt, pepper and herbs and continue to simmer for 15 minutes while you get your jars sterilised. Blend again if desired.
3. Bottle, freeze or use fresh – the choice is yours. I prefer to thicken my sauce with Cornflour, if necessary, when I add it to the final dish but obviously omit for the gluten free guest.

The Art of Preserving

Preserving Beetroot

When beetroot is in season, there is nothing sweeter. They are dead easy to grow and the leaves are great in salads or steamed with a small piece of lemon.

PREPARING THE BEETROOT:

When harvesting, make sure you leave the top part of the stem (just above the bulb) intact; otherwise when you boil them, their beautiful colour will leach out into the water if you have cut them too low. The same goes for any long roots – leave them intact, but wash them really well without scoring the skin. It's best not to let them grow too big as they will be a bit 'hairy' in the middle after they are cooked and this will compromise their flavour and texture.

Then simply place your beetroot in a large saucepan and cover with cold water. Bring them to the boil and then simmer them until tender. The time this takes will depend on their size but you can check by sticking in a skewer.

When they are cold, don the rubber gloves and carefully peel and slice them, ready for preserving.

Lisa's Preserved Beetroot (GF)

You will need to vary the amount of mixture that you make, depending on the size and how many beetroot you have to preserve, so this is simply a guideline. The idea is that the vinegar mixture should cover the beetroot in the jar. You will use about 200 mls of vinegar mixture per 520 gram gherkin jar which has been pre-packed with beetroot.

INGREDIENTS:

- Boiled beetroot (7-8 large) peeled and sliced (or cut into wedges)
- Sterilised jars and lids
- 4 cups of sugar (half brown if you have it – cane sugar is gluten free)
- 8 cups of vinegar
- Some black peppercorns
- A sprinkle of ground cloves
- A sprinkle of cinnamon
- A sprinkle of nutmeg
- 2 bay leaves, discard before bottling
- A few sprigs of fresh mint

98   The Art of Preserving

METHOD:

1. Combine the sugar, vinegar and spices in a large saucepan and bring to the boil, stirring until the sugar is dissolved.
2. Carefully add your sliced beetroot and bring back to the boil.
3. Throw in some sprigs of mint.
4. Using tongs; place your beetroot into your jars and then using a glass jug, cover them with the vinegar mixture.
5. Seal and store. This recipe makes enough to fill approximately 8 gherkin jars. As with most preserves, try and resist the urge to eat them straight away. Store them in a cool, dark place and once opened, refrigerate.

Easy Lemon Curd Spread

This spread can also be used as a filling for tarts or lemon meringue pies, as a pancake topping or even just spread on toast. If your jars are sterilised properly, it should keep unopened in a cool, dark place for several months. Once the jar is opened, keep it in the fridge and use within a couple of weeks or when mould starts to form – whichever comes first.

INGREDIENTS:

- 125 grams of butter, cut into small cubes
- 3 eggs, whisked well
- The zest of one lemon
- ¾ cup of fresh lemon juice
- ¾ cup of sugar (cane sugar is gluten free)
- Sterilised jars and lids for longer term storage

METHOD:

1. Place all ingredients in a large saucepan.
2. Heat on medium and whisk continually until the mixture thickens. Do not allow to boil.
3. Pour immediately into warm, sterilised jars. Store in a cool, dark place.

The Art of Preserving

Preserved Fruit – Without the Fancy Equipment (GF)

INGREDIENTS:

- The desired amount of fruit of your choice, peeled (if necessary) stones removed and cut into halves, quarters or even eighths (eg apricots, pears, peaches). You should choose ripe fruit and remove any imperfections. Firm fruit may need a little water added if it doesn't seem juicy enough when cooking.
- The amount of sugar of your choice. Really ripe fruit will not need much, whilst firmer fruit will need more. Some sugar helps to stop the fruit from discolouring and can help extend the life of your preserves.
- Juice of half a lemon
- Sterilised jars/lids

METHOD:

1. Bring your fruit, sugar and water (if needed) to the boil in a large saucepan.
2. Reduce and simmer for 10-15 minutes or so, or until the fruit is tender.
3. Using a ladle or heat proof jug, carefully fill the warm sterilised jars with the hot fruit and seal immediately.
4. Allow to cool before labelling and storing in a cool, dark place. It should keep indefinitely. Refrigerate after opening.

PRESERVING FOOTNOTE:

For preserving fruits and vegetables on a larger scale it is well worth investing in a commercially bought electric preserving outfit, as these are properly designed and thermostatically controlled, ensuring a perfect preserve every time.

Such kits use a 'hot water bath' method and usually require specially designed preserving jars with rubber rings and clips. The unit itself is not unlike an urn inside as it has a raised bottom so that the jars do not come in direct contact with the element. The preserves are then covered in cold water, brought to the correct temperature and processed for the required amount of time depending on the produce being used. This method gives you double insurance against any bacteria as all of the items involved come to a high temperature.

Although you can simulate this process yourself by using a deep saucepan with a raised base and thermometer, if it is something you are likely to be doing again, just go out and pay the money for the real deal. Better still, split the cost with a friend and share it.

Dehydrating (or drying) food is another popular method of preserving. As with bottled produce, dried foods can be kept for long periods of time if stored in a cool, dark place. I usually just cut up my fruit for drying and drop it into a bowl of water which has had the juice of a lemon and a little bit of dissolved sugar added to it. This helps stop any discolouration. From there I simply drain it and place it on the drying racks. If purchasing a dehydrator I highly recommend that you buy one that has a variable thermostat and to which you can add extra trays when and if you need them.

Note: Always discard any bottled preserve which has an unusual colour, smell or bubbly appearance in the jar, as these are all signs that the produce did not seal properly or that your sterilisation process may not have been successful. There can be significant health risks associated with eating such products. And finally, if re-using 'pop- top' jars, make sure the lid has depressed in the centre when the preserve has cooled down, otherwise it has not sealed properly and will need to be used straight away.

Festive Fare

Everything you need to know to get you through the biggest culinary day of the year

As I type the Festive Fare section, Christmas is only a few days away. I love absolutely everything about Christmas – except for my bank balance. But, as they say, you can't take it with you!

I love the fact (secretly) that my family hates my Christmas music with a passion – it gives us all something to laugh about; I love grilled ham, cheese, tomato and cranberry croissants with orange juice for breakfast; I love sharing family meals of roast turkey and crunchy potatoes, with all the trimmings; I love that it's a time to think about those who we have lost, as they are never really far away; I love the games and fun times with family and friends; and I love the fact that we all severely overestimate the amount of food and drink our bodies can consume, and collapse in a heap on the nearest couch at about 3 pm, where we lay in wait for our second wind. Well it seems that after 40 we need to.

In this section I aim to demystify some of the traditional aspects of Festive Fare.

How to Stuff a Turkey

Growing up on a farm, turkey was a part of our staple diet for as long as I can remember, and even before my time when my Grandmother used to cook them in her wood stove but many people are afraid of cooking this flavoursome bird. One's first thought is that it smells quite different to chicken and this is quite correct as it has a quite gamey aroma by comparison.

What I add to my poultry stuffing often depends on how I am basting my meat. For example, if I am basting with apricot jam I might include diced apricots and almonds (which go well with apricots) in my mixture. This recipe is just an idea but you can experiment with your own flavours, nuts and herbs.

The amount you need also depends on the size of the turkey or piece of meat you are stuffing (not to be confused with stuffing up). This recipe uses a food processor that will save you lots of time; otherwise you will need some patience and good knife skills.

INGREDIENTS:

- ½-¾ loaf of fresh bread-crumbs (I prefer to use wholemeal or grainy and you can buy gluten free varieties buzzed up yourself in the food processor)
- 1 large onion, peeled and roughly cut
- A decent cup full of dried apricots (other suggestions are cranberries or prunes- which will keep you regular if nothing else)
- A cup of roughly chopped almonds (pine nuts are also nice in stuffing)
- A large handful of finely diced fresh herbs such as rosemary, thyme, sage, oregano (or you could substitute with 2 tablespoons of dried mixed herbs)
- Orange juice to bind (or you can use water)
- A good few grinds of salt and black pepper

METHOD:

1. Place the bread in batches into your food processor and process until they become reasonably fine bread crumbs. Remove to a large bowl.
2. Process the onion, dried fruit and nuts. If using pine nuts, leave them whole.
3. Add the fresh herbs to the processor and pulse for a few seconds. Mmm – the smell of those fresh herbs!
4. Add this mix to the bread crumbs, along with the salt and pepper and stir well.
5. Add just enough orange juice to the mixture so it will hold together when squeezed.
6. Push handfuls of stuffing into the well-rinsed cavity of your bird - the turkey that is! Try to fill it fairly firmly so there are not too many air pockets.
7. Baste the bird and cook for the required amount of time.

Cooking the Turkey

- Rinse the inside cavity and outside of the turkey under clean, running water and only stuff the turkey immediately before roasting. Don't over fill, as the stuffing will expand slightly when cooked. **Make sure the turkey is completely defrosted before proceeding.**
- Tie the legs together with non-plastic-coated string, encompassing the tail as well.
- Place some small pieces of foil (shiny side in) over the wings and lower drumsticks of the bird as these cook much faster and will dry out too much otherwise.
- Baste the bird with oil, jam, spices etc and place in a shallow roasting pan. My family always used to lay a couple of rashers of bacon over the breast of the turkey. This served to both moisten and flavour the bird nicely. Cover the bird with some large pieces of foil – shiny side in.
- It is important at this stage to know the weight of the stuffed bird to help you determine the cooking time. Cook the turkey in an oven or BBQ kettle at 170-180°C. Temp inside the bird must reach at least 80°C (in the leg crevice and breast of the bird) and 78°C (inside the stuffing) for food safety.
- Basting of any juices or marinades can be done at intervals throughout the cooking time, re-covering with the foil afterwards to stop the bird from drying out.
- Browning of the bird should only take place in the last 30 minutes or so of cooking at which time the main foil covering the bird can be removed.
- To check if cooked, insert a sharp knife into the crevice between the back leg and the body and pierce well into the meat. The juices should run clear. **If there is any hint of pink in the juice, the turkey is not properly cooked and needs to continue baking.**
- When cooked, remove from the oven and leave to rest on a large serving platter or tray and cover with foil (shiny side in). Rest for 15 minutes or so before carving.
- Don't forget to drain the fat off your pan juices, add some water, a gluten free chicken stock cube, salt, pepper and some Cornflour and stir until it boils for delicious gravy.

Approximate cooking times:

WEIGHT	NO STUFFING	STUFFED BIRD
4.5 - 8.5 kg (10-18 lbs)	3 - 3½ hours	3¾ - 4½ hours
8.5 - 10 kg (18-22 lbs)	3½ - 4 hours	4½ - 5 hours
10 - 11 kg (22-24 lbs)	4 - 4½ hours	5 - 5½ hours
11 - 13.5 kg (24-29 lbs)	4½ - 5 hours	5½ - 6¼ hours

Fifi's Roast Pork with Crispy Crackling (GF)

Delicious roast pork can be prepared either in the oven or your BBQ kettle.

INGREDIENTS:

- A pork roast, the size of your choice
- Olive oil
- Salt

METHOD:

1. Remove plastic cover – DA!
2. Pat the pork dry with paper towel.
3. Use a sharp pointed knife to score the rind on the upper side of the pork. This will allow more heat into the skin to create a crisper rind and crackling.
4. Massage the pork roast well with olive oil. Now don't get kinky on me!
5. Sprinkle liberally with plenty of salt. Look that up in the Dictionary if you don't know what liberally means! Rub the salt well into the skin.
6. Preheat the oven to 230°C and place the pork in a greased baking dish. Cook on this high heat for 15-20 minutes until your meat is 'sizzling' and your crackle is 'cracklin'.
7. After 20 minutes reduce the heat of your oven to approximately 150°C – the idea now being to slow cook your meat to ensure it is tender and moist.
8. Return your oven to a higher heat for the final 20 minutes or so of cooking.

Note: The cooking time is completely dependent on the size of your roast, but when you prick it with a skewer, the juices should run clear. Also, don't waste your baked ham rinds as these can be cooked up for extra crackling. Score and salt as previously mentioned and cook until crispy.

A Guide to Baking Hams

There are 101 different glaze recipes for ham. In the past, I have used dried fruits, pineapple rings, jams etc. Here Sara gives you a guide to the basic principles of a baked ham which looks amazing displayed on an inexpensive rack bought from a discount shop. Unless marked otherwise, many hams and deli meats contain gluten so be careful if this may apply to your guests.

INGREDIENTS:

- 1 picnic ham
- ½ cup of honey, melted
- Whole cloves to decorate

MUSTARD HONEY GLAZE INGREDIENTS:

- 1 cup of apricot nectar
- ¼ cup of firmly packed brown sugar
- 1 tablespoon of Dijon mustard
- ¼ cup of orange juice
- ½ cup of apricot jam

METHOD:

1. Preheat the oven to 180°C.
2. Place glaze ingredients in a small saucepan and stir over a low heat. Do not allow it to boil. Strain well using a metal sieve to remove the solids.
3. Carefully cut through the rind, making a pattern near the shank end with your knife.
4. Make another incision with your knife around the edge of the area on the ham that you wish to decorate (the top).
5. At the big end of the ham, begin carefully separating the rind from the meat, trying hard to keep the layer of white fat intact on the ham. Use your thumb and fingers to help separate the two.
6. Gently score a pattern into the fatty layer and then decorate with the cloves.
7. Place the ham on a wire rack in a large baking dish and cover the bone end with some foil to prevent over cooking.
8. Brush the surface carefully with honey and bake uncovered for 20 minutes.
9. At this stage you begin to baste your ham with the mustard glaze, two or three times over the next 20 minutes, until nice and golden.
10. Tie a ribbon around the top and serve hot or cold.

Note: Ham rinds can be frozen for later use, just make sure you dry them thoroughly with paper towel before cooking.

Also, when you think you are finished with the ham bone, don't waste it on the animals; pop it in the freezer to use as soup stock down the track. That is if you can prise it away!

Festive Fare

Fifi's Naughty but Nice Roast Potatoes (GF)

I call them Naughty but Nice because one wouldn't usually partake in eating so much fat and salt – but what the hell – it's Christmas! To the right is a disclaimer against any heart attacks which may happen on Christmas Day! My family looks forward to a feed of Aunty Fifi's potatoes for the next 364 days of the year.

INGREDIENTS:

- The desired number of peeled and quartered potatoes of your choice. The best varieties of roasting potatoes include King Edward, Royal Blue, Coliban, Delaware and Sebago.
- Duck fat or dripping (this can be purchased at most large supermarkets but if you cannot get either of these, just use extra oil)
- Olive oil
- Salt

METHOD:

1. Preheat the oven or BBQ kettle to a high heat – around 220°C.
2. Peel and quarter your spuds. Hopefully you can find a mate to help you if you've got heaps to do.
3. Line a large roasting dish with baking paper.
4. Slosh a generous amount of olive oil in the bottom along with a similar amount of duck fat or dripping.
5. Throw the spuds in on top, stirring to coat, and give another slosh of oil over the top.
6. Sprinkle generously with ground rock salt and place into the hot oven.
7. Cook for approximately 20 minutes on this high heat. Remove from oven and give the tray a good wriggle to loosen any stuck spuds.
8. Reduce the heat to 150°C and return the potatoes. Continue to cook for approximately 1 hour, turning occasionally, until cooked through.
9. As a final step, return the heat to high for the last 30 minutes or so, salting once again; just in case you thought your arteries were not hard enough already. Drain well.

Lisa's Cauliflower and Broccoli Au Gratin

My nephew (who is not a big veggie eater) tells me he looks forward to my Au Gratin for Christmas every year, so I like to think I am doing my bit towards his annual vegetable intake. With Christmas being such a busy time I always prepare it a couple of days beforehand so it is ready to whack in the oven to either fully cook or reheat on the big day.

INGREDIENTS:

- Desired amount of cauliflower, washed and cut into flowerets
- Desired amount of broccoli, washed and cut into flowerets

WHITE SAUCE INGREDIENTS:

- 1 onion, peeled and very finely diced
- 1 decent tablespoon of butter
- 2 litres of milk
- ½-¾ cup of Plain flour (you can use gluten free flour)
- 2-3 pinches of nutmeg
- ½ cup of grated Parmesan cheese
- Good grind of salt and pepper

CRUNCHY CHEESE TOPPING:

- 2 cups of wholemeal bread crumbs (you can buy gluten free bread crumbs or rice crumbs)
- Some grated cheese
- Salt and pepper
- Ground paprika, optional

METHOD:

1. Preheat the oven to 180°C.
2. Wash the cauliflower and broccoli and place batches in a microwave safe dish and cook on HIGH until tender, stirring once half way. Continue until all cooked.
3. Melt the butter in a large saucepan and add the onion. Fry until transparent but not golden.
4. Pour in 1½ litres of the milk and the nutmeg. Reduce your element to a medium heat as you don't want your milk to boil.
5. Place the remaining milk and flour in a large glass jar (or similar) with a tight fitting lid. Shake the daylights out of it until there are no lumps.
6. Stir the flour mixture into the saucepan and continue to stir until the sauce begins to thicken, adding more flour if the sauce is too thin. Try not to let it boil as it will bubble up over the saucepan causing you to swear profusely.
7. Remove from the heat and add the grated cheese, salt and pepper.
8. Arrange your broccoli and cauliflower in a shallow baking dish.
9. Pour the sauce evenly over the top.
10. Sprinkle over the bread crumbs and then the grated cheese, finishing with the salt, pepper and paprika. Cover with foil (shiny side towards the food).
11. Bake for approximately half an hour before removing the foil for the last 15 minutes or so to allow the top to brown up nicely.

Mum's Traditional Steamed Christmas Pudding

Thinking of fruit pudding still brings a tear to my eye, as it was always my mum's job to provide the dessert for Christmas.

Back in the days when it was safe to do so (or maybe we just thought it was safe) she would diligently boil up the coins and poke them into the pudding just before serving, and we would sit and wait in anticipation of being the lucky one to receive the big twenty cent coin. Oh those were the days!

For quite a few years after her death, I could not bring myself to make a Christmas pudding, but this year I brought mum's recipe back to life. I believe in fact, that it actually came from her Aunty, so it's very, very old indeed. I'm sure that there are quicker recipes out there, but for me, Christmas is very much about tradition.

As with most recipes, you can substitute the fruit of your choice, the aim is to keep the quantities the same.

As steamed puddings have not been part of my normal cooking line-up to date, I went to a second hand shop and picked up a pudding tin for $1.50. It even had the string still attached from which to hang the wooden spoon – bonus!

INGREDIENTS:

- 2 cups of Self Raising flour
- 1 cup of sultanas
- 1 cup of raisins
- 1 cup of currants
- 1 cup of slivered almonds
- 1 cup of cold water
- 1 cup of hot water
- 1 cup of sugar
- 1 cup of sweet sherry or brandy
- 2 small tablespoons of butter
- 2 small tablespoons of bi-carb soda
- 2 heaped teaspoons of mixed spice

METHOD:

1. Place the butter in a large bowl and pour the hot water over the butter, stirring until melted.
2. Dissolve the bi-carb soda in the cold water and add to the bowl along with all of the other ingredients. Mix well (the mixture will appear quite sloppy). Cover and refrigerate overnight or for several hours.
3. The next day (at which time you will notice that it has thickened quite a lot) place the mixture into a very well-greased 4-5 cup capacity pudding tin. Don't forget to grease the lid too before putting it on and firmly securing. You could also use an old fashioned ceramic bowl that is a similar shape. If doing this, you need to cover the pudding with baking paper and then foil and tie string around it to make it water tight. You will also need to fashion a handle out of string for the steaming process.

TO STEAM THE PUDDING:

1. Place the sealed pudding tin into a large saucepan.
2. Use a wooden spoon and some string to suspend your pudding so the base is not touching the bottom of the saucepan. This will ensure that it does not burn on the bottom.
3. Carefully fill the saucepan with cold water, three quarters of the way up the side of your pudding tin.
4. Bring to the boil and reduce to simmer, checking water levels and adding more water from time to time. I add boiling water from the kettle so that it remains simmering. Steam for 4 hours. Allow to cool before carefully removing and turning upside down onto your serving plate.

Note: To reheat you can simply turn it out onto a plate and zap it for a few minutes on a MEDIUM heat in the microwave or place the pudding back in its tin in the boiling water for 25–30 minutes.

Brandy Custard

This is a slight variation of my normal custard recipe with grog included. This makes 4 cups of custard.

INGREDIENTS:

- 3½ cups of milk
- 6 tablespoons of sugar
- 5 rounded tablespoons of custard powder
- ½ cup of Brandy

METHOD:

1. Heat 2½ cups of the milk along with the sugar in a good-sized saucepan over a medium heat.
2. Place the remaining cup of milk and the custard powder in a large jar, put the lid on and shake the beejeebers out of it to remove any lumps.
3. Pour into the warm milk mixture and continue to stir with a whisk or wooden spoon until it thickens, making sure you don't let it boil.
4. Remove from the heat and stir in the Brandy.

Note: Adjust the amount of custard powder and milk (and Brandy) to your personal preference in regards to thickness and inebriation!

Festive Fare

Nana's Sweet Marshmallow and Mandarin Salad

Christmas is full of surprises and none more so than Nana's signature salad. Like my Christmas music, Nana's salad always brings up some family debate – some positively love it with the savoury treats of Christmas, whilst others think it belongs in the sweets category. Either way, it's a little bit different and a very colourful addition to the festive table. If you love marshmallows, this could be for you.

INGREDIENTS:

- 1 cup of mandarin flesh, cut into small segments
- 1 cup of pineapple pieces, well drained
- 1 cup of desiccated coconut
- 1 cup of white marshmallows, chopped fairly finely
- 1 cup of cream

METHOD:

1. Place the first four ingredients in a bowl and stir in the cream.
2. Transfer to your serving bowl and decorate with some extra pineapple slices and pink marshmallows. Refrigerate until ready to serve.

Lili's Prawn Pizza Dip

Even though this recipe uses some reduced fat products, I can't tell you that it's not harsh on the waistline. This being said, it's a pretty 'specky' looking dip for a special occasion and it will still work with other seafood. I often bring it out on Christmas day. You sort of build this dip up from the bottom like a pizza.

INGREDIENTS:

- 1 tub of light cream cheese (or perhaps substitute low fat cottage cheese)
- ¾ cup of reduced fat Thousand Island sauce
- 1 cup of grated fat reduced cheese
- 4 large sweet spiced gherkins, finely diced
- 4 large sweet pickled onions, finely diced
- ½ red capsicum, finely diced
- Some freshly cooked and peeled prawns, roughly chopped (leave a couple whole for decorating)

METHOD:

1. Spread the cream cheese evenly over your serving plate.
2. Cover with the Thousand Island sauce.
3. Sprinkle over most of the cheese, gherkins, capsicum and onion.
4. Push the fresh prawns down into the base and then top with a little extra cheese.
5. Serve with corn chips or fresh veggie sticks.

Aunty D's Easy As Fruit Cake

This has got to be the easiest fruit cake ever and my Aunty swears that it keeps for months in the fridge.

INGREDIENTS/METHOD:

- 1 kg of mixed dried fruit of your choice
- 2 cups of orange juice, fresh or bought

Soak overnight or for several hours and then add:

- 2 cups of Self Raising flour and stir well

Pour into a greased and lined 20 cm square cake tin. I throw a few almonds on top of mine. Bake at 160°C for 1 hour and 40 minutes. Alternatively you can cook it in a 25 cm x 30 cm slice tin in which case it would only take around 50 minutes to cook. Cut into squares when cool.

Note: *If the cake is getting too brown on top, turn down the heat a little.*

Christmas Chews

This recipe is based on another one from my dear Aunty D and is so easy it's child's play - just watch them when it comes to the grog! These keep for ages and are nice and chewy.

INGREDIENTS:

- 1 cup of Self Raising flour
- 1¾ cups mixed dried fruit of your choice (1 x 225 g packet of fruit medley)
- ¼ cup of shelled pistachios, roughly chopped (you can buy them already shelled if you are not a patient person)
- 1 tin of condensed milk
- A small splash of Brandy or Rum
- Some slivered almonds

METHOD:

1. Preheat the oven to 160°C.
2. Combine all ingredients (except for almonds) in a bowl and mix well.
3. Place mixture into a greased and lined 30 cm x 20 cm slice tin and sprinkle with the almonds.
4. Place the tray on the middle rack of your oven and bake for approximately 25 minutes. When cool, cut into squares.

Festive Fare

One Pan Chocolate Brownies

As uninteresting as these may look, I guarantee it will take a supreme amount of will power to stop at one. Take some comfort in knowing that there are more health benefits in dark chocolate (weight loss not necessarily one of them) than some other forms.

INGREDIENTS:

- 1 x 200 gram block of dark chocolate with nuts in it, broken into individual squares. You are allowed to have one square just to make sure the quality is OK.
- 250 grams of butter, cut into chunks
- 2 cups of sugar
- 4 eggs
- 2 cups of Plain flour
- ½ teaspoon of salt
- A squirt of vanilla essence
- A small handful of walnuts or pecans (if your chocolate did not contain nuts)

METHOD:

1. Preheat the oven to 170°C.
2. Place the butter in either a large microwave safe jug or a medium sized saucepan. Heat the butter until it has dissolved and is bubbling.
3. Remove from heat and stir in the chocolate and sugar with a wooden spoon. Let sit for 2-3 minutes then stir until chocolate is all melted.
4. Add the nuts and salt to the chocolate mixture.
5. Meanwhile crack the eggs into a cup and whisk lightly with a fork. Stir in the vanilla.
6. Gradually stir the beaten egg and flour into the chocolate mixture.
7. Grease and line a lamington style tray with sides (or a 24 cm square cake tin) and pour in the mixture. If you use a cake tin with higher sides like I do, you will need to line it well with baking paper as this will help you to lift it out in one piece without breaking the slice. A proper lamington tray is much easier to tip upside down and remove. The mixture may appear a bit grainy but this is normal.
8. Lick the bowl, if you are that way inclined.
9. Bake for approximately 40-45 minutes, until the top is 'set'.
10. Remove from the oven and let sit in the tin for a few minutes before slicing into around 25 respectable sized squares. Don't be surprised if the mixture still seems a bit wobbly when you get it out of the oven as it will firm more when it cools.
11. Try and let it cool completely before tasting and then brush your teeth immediately after.

Note: If you like your brownies chewier, reduce the cooking time by a few minutes.

Index

Prenuptials to Cooking

Nice Rice, 1
Fail-Safe Rice (GF), 2
Gluten Free Guest, 2
Cleaning Out the Fridge, 4
Taking Stock of Stock Cubes, 4
Setting the Table, 5
How to Excel at Garage Sales, 7
A Guide to Box Gardening, 8
Indoor Seed Propagation, 12

Herbing it Up!

Cooking with Fresh Herbs, 14
Glossary of Herbs, 14
Fresh Herb Pesto (GF), 17
Chargrilled Vegetables in Herb Oil (GF), 17
Fresh Zucchini and Spinach Soup with Coriander (GF), 18
Easy Egg Frittata with Fresh Herbs (GF), 19
Mustard Herb Pilaf (GF), 20
Couscous Tabouli with Fresh Parsley, 21
Rustic Potato Salad with Rosemary (GF), 22

How to Masta Pasta

Different Types of Pasta, 24
Basic Pasta Making, 25
Cooking Fresh Pasta, 27
Lemon Cream Fettuccine with Tuna, 27
Spinach and Ricotta Ravioli with (Not Quite) Burnt Butter Sage, 28
Chook's Seafood Marinara, 29
Roasted Pumpkin and Spinach Lasagne, 30

Bread Making for Beginners

Basic Guides and Tips, 32
Basic Bread Dough, 32
Basic Pide Bread, 33
Turkish Pizza Pide, 33
Plaited Bread Sticks, 34
Pear and Pancetta Pizza with Walnuts and Honey, 35
Hot Cross Buns, 36

Seafood Made Simple

From the Ocean to the Table, 38
How to Fillet a Fish, 39
Lemon and Dill Crusted Whiting, 40
Snapper Italiane (GF), 41
Neil's Smoked Snook, 42
Marinated Tuna Steaks (GF), 43
Mango Salsa (GF), 43
Mango Chutney Glaze (GF), 44
How to Butterfly Fillet Garfish, 44
Beer Battered Garfish, 45
Tender Squid Every Time, 46
How to Clean Calamari, 46
Salt and Pepper Squid, 48
How to Shuck an Oyster, 48
Oysters Kilpatrick, 49
Crabs, 50
Tying Crabs, 51
Cleaning Crabs, 52
Beer Steamed Blueys, 53
How to Peel a Prawn, 54
Specky Prawn and Nectarine Salad (GF), 55
Prawn Laksa, 56
How to Cook and Clean Yabbies, 56
Sam's Pickled Yabbies (GF), 57
Zombie's Tips for Cooking Crayfish, 58

Camping Capers

What Type of Camper are You?, 60
Food Tips when Camping, 62
The Humble Ironing Board, 64
Getting Gassed and Connected, 65
Lighting Up, 66
A Word on Fire Lighting, 67
Tips on Fire Lighting, 67
Fire Safety, 67
Camp Oven Cooking, 68
Hearty Pumpkin Soup with Fresh Rosemary and Coriander (GF), 69
Camp Oven Apricot Chicken with Rosemary (GF), 70
Jaffles, 71
The Bung it on Barbie, 71
Beer Bread, 72
Damper, 73
Apple Fritters, 73
Big A*se Golden Syrup Dumplings, 74
Lemonade Scones, 74

The Meaty Bits

A Butcher's Guide to Choosing Your Meat, 76
A Guide to Cooking Steak, 77
Roy's Finger Test, 77
A Guide to Marinating, 78
Chicken – Teriyaki Marinade (GF), 78
Chicken – Asian Satay Sauce (GF), 78
Chicken – Orange and Tarragon Marinade, 79
Pork – Honey Mustard Marinade with a Tarragon Twist (GF), 79
Pork – Plum Sauce, 79
Beef – Basic Red Wine Marinade (GF), 80
Beef – Beef 'N' Beer Marinade, 80
Lamb – Jam and Yogurt Marinade (GF), 81
Lamb – Sweet Chilli Rub, 81
Meaty Recipes, 82
Lili's Lamb Parmi, 82
Lozza's Lamb Chops with Fancy Sauce (GF), 83
Slow Cooked Moroccan Lamb (GF), 84
Lisa's Hurry Curry with Rice (GF), 85
Quick Chick Curry (GF), 86

The Art of Preserving

Sterilising Jam Jars and Metal Lids, 88
General Preserving and Jam Making Tips, 89
Strawberry and Pineapple Jam (GF), 91
Sweet Mango Chutney (GF), 92
Zucchini and Apple Relish (GF), 93
Quintessential Quince Paste (GF), 94
Lisa's Sweet Pickles (GF), 95
Ronda's Homemade Sauce (GF), 96
Pasta Sauce with Red Wine (GF), 97
Preserving Beetroot, 98
Lisa's Preserved Beetroot (GF), 98
Easy Lemon Curd Spread, 99
Preserved Fruit (GF), 100

Festive Fare

How to Stuff a Turkey, 102
Cooking the Turkey, 103
Fifi's Roast Pork with Crispy Crackling (GF), 104
A Guide to Baking Hams, 105
Fifi's Naughty but Nice Roast Potatoes (GF), 106
Lisa's Cauliflower and Broccoli Au Gratin, 107
Mum's Traditional Steamed Christmas Pudding, 108
Brandy Custard, 109
Nana's Sweet Marshmallow and Mandarin Salad, 110
Lili's Prawn Pizza Dip, 110
Aunty D's Easy As Fruit Cake, 111
Christmas Chews, 111
One Pan Chocolate Brownies, 112

Glossary of Aussie Slang #2

Ain't	Are not, or is not
Anal	Not in its true sense (as we all know what that means) but when it comes to people – uptight and downright painful (not in the anal area – though some would describe 'anal' behaviour as being a pain in the a*se)
Beejeebers	Living daylights, the heck out of etc
Behind the 8 Ball	Left behind, unorganised or disadvantaged
Bob's Your Uncle	(He's probably not) but I have absolutely no idea where this came from but it basically means – she'll be right mate
Bottle O	Drive-through liquor store
Chooks	Chickens
Cold Shoulder	If you give someone the 'cold shoulder' you are usually ignoring them because they have done something wrong
Coldie	Nice cold beverage – usually a beer
Couch Potato	Someone who spends too much time on the couch and whose bum is starting to resemble a potato (or in some cases a whole sack)
Crabs	Also known as an unfortunate infestation in the nether regions!
Crank Up	Start or get going
Crook	Sick
DA	Dumb A*se or fool
Dead Horse	Tomato sauce – don't ask me why – just rhyming slang!
Don't Shoot the Messenger	Don't blame the person who told you – he was just passing it on
Down the Track	Later on or in the future
Dud	Reject, flop
Eat Your Words	Take back what you said as you have already regretted saying it
Fandangled	Fancy
Fellas	Blokes, men, guys
First in Best Dressed	Its the quick or the dead, or otherwise miss out
Flop	If something is a 'flop' it is a failure
Forking Out	Paying for, or giving up something 'wanted'
Go to town	Have a good time, go your hardest, don't hold back
Grog	Alcohol
Have a Crack	Have a go
Heads Up	Information

Glossary of Aussie Slang #2...

Hit and Miss	Unreliable
Kill Two Birds with One Stone	Achieving two things at the same time – multi-tasking
Kinky	A little bit weird and bordering on inappropriate!
Long Neck	Old fashioned big bottle of beer or ale
Lost the Plot	The state you get in when everything turns pear shaped (see below) and when you are likely to commit highly irrational acts
Machine-gun Bum	Diarrhoea or a good old fashioned dose of the sh*ts
Munchies	If you have a case of the 'munchies' you are very hungry and need something to nibble on
Neck of the Woods	In your district or area
Off the Hook	Released from obligation
OMG!	Oh my God/goodness/golly gosh
Pear Shaped	Means things have gone horribly wrong
Reckons	Thinks
Rocks Up	Arrives
Rookie	Novice or inexperienced person or act
RSI	Not actually slang, but stands for repetitive strain injury
Side Tracked	Diverting your attention somewhere other than where it was intended
Snaggy	A 'snag' (not to be confused with sausage) is a Sensitive New Age Guy, so if someone is 'snaggy' they are a modern guy or someone who may not be too keen on getting their hands dirty (A disgrace to the male race I say)
Threw in the Towel	Gave up
Two Cents Worth	Opinion – whether it is welcomed or not
W.C.	Water closet, windy corner, dunny, toilet, lavatory

About The Author

The Aussie Dumb A*se Cookbook 2 'A Hunter and Gatherer's Guide' is Lisa's second instalment in her quest to encourage people to 'have a crack' in the kitchen, and this time touches on the garden too.

Since the release of The Aussie Dumb A*se Cookbook (the essential guide to cooking and survival for the domestically challenged!) in 2009, Lisa has taken on a Specialist Kitchen role as part of a National Stephanie Alexander Kitchen Garden Program at her local school.

"I am totally in love with seeing, hearing and sharing in the excitement of growing and preparing fresh food. Oh there have been plenty of failures along the way but the power of modelling good food practices to others has been really highlighted for me with the growing and sharing of knowledge with the children I work with. Some of these are as young as five, so this proves to me that you are never too young (or old) to learn new ways of doing things.

*This Hunter and Gatherer's Guide is a combination of many trials and errors on my own learning adventure, all of which have been taste tested and given the seal of approval by my family, friends and loved ones (in other words the important people). That makes it a proven 'Dumb A*se' proof guide for the novice!"*

Happy cooking,

Lisa

CPSIA information can be obtained
at www.ICGtesting.com
Printed in the USA
BVHW020947190820
586812BV00017B/1475